# EXPLORATIONS

*STUDIES IN CULTURE AND COMMUNICATION*

**VOLUME 3**

*Edited by Edmund Carpenter and
Marshall McLuhan*

WIPF & STOCK · Eugene, Oregon

Wipf and Stock Publishers
199 W 8th Ave, Suite 3
Eugene, OR 97401

Explorations 3
Studies in Culture and Communication
By Carpenter, E S and Easterbrook, W T
Copyright©1954, Edmund S. Carpenter & Marshall McLuhan Estates
ISBN 13: 978-1-62032-429-5
Publication date 9/27/2016
Previously published by University of Toronto, 1954

This is an anniversary new edition of the eight co–edited issues of Explorations, with annotations by Michael Darroch and Janine Marchessault, in conjunction with students and researchers at the University of Windsor and York University, Canada. Research for the annotated editions was made possible by a grant from the Social Sciences and Humanities Research Council of Canada. Additional research was provided by Lorraine Spiess in conjunction with the Estate of Edmund Carpenter. Permissions research was provided by Jonathan McKenzie. This republication project was a joint initiative undertaken by the estates of Marshall McLuhan and Edmund Carpenter.

Funding for Issues 1–6 (1953–1956) was originally provided by a grant from the Ford Foundation's Behavioral Sciences Program. Issues 7–8 (1957) were sponsored by the Telegram of Toronto.

Typography for Issue 1 was designed and printed by Rous & Mann Press Limited, Toronto. The cover of Issue 7 and the cover and typography of Issue 8 were designed by Harley Parker and printed courtesy of the University of Toronto Press. Please see individual issues for further notes on contributors and acknowledgements.

## EXPLORATIONS . . .

is designed, not as a permanent reference journal that embalms truth for posterity, but as a publication that explores and searches and questions.

We envisage a series that will cut across the humanities and social sciences by treating them as a continuum. We believe anthropology and communication are approaches, not bodies of data, and that within each the four winds of the humanities, the physical, the biological and the social sciences intermingle to form a science of man.

### Volumes 1 through 6:

Editor:
    E. S. Carpenter
Associate Editors:
    W. T. Easterbrook
    H. M. McLuhan
    J. Tyrwhitt
    D. C. Williams

Address all correspondence to EXPLORATIONS
 University of Toronto
 Toronto, Canada

### Volumes 7 & 8:

Editors:
    Edmund Carpenter
    Marshall McLuhan

Sponsor Telegram of Toronto
Publisher University of Toronto

*August 1954*

# Explorations, 1953–57

# Foreword to the Eight-Volume Series of the 2016 Edition, Volumes 2–8

*(The main Introduction to this series is in Volume One)*

Michael Darroch (University of Windsor) and
Janine Marchessault (York University)

*Explorations* was an experimental interdisciplinary publication led by faculty and graduate students at the University of Toronto in which the media theorist Marshall McLuhan and the radical anthropologist Edmund Carpenter formulated their most striking insights about new media in the electric age. The journal served to disseminate some of the insights and experiments of the Culture and Communications graduate seminar (1953–55), an innovative media think tank of the 1950s. The eight coedited issues of *Explorations* are republished here for the first time since their original printing in the 1950s.

The Explorations research group aimed to develop a "field approach" to the study of new media and communication. While inspired by a postwar, modernist discourse of universality, no single mode of research was dominant. By their own account, the team sought "an area of mutually supporting insights in a critique of the methods of study in Economics, Psychology, English, Anthropology, and Town Planning."[1] *Explorations* published writings by group

---

1. Herbert Marshall McLuhan Fonds, held in Library and Archives Canada (LAC) in Ottawa. Further references to the McLuhan Fonds will be identified as LAC followed by the call number MG 31, D 156, the volume number, and the folder number (here: LAC MG 31, D 156, 145, 35).

members along with contributions on topics ranging from ethnolinguistics to economic theory, from art and design to developmental psychology, from psychoanalysis to nursery rhymes and bawdy ballads, from urban theory to electronic media. The journal treated culture, and cultural studies, as a landscape of experiences and knowledge. An experimental space in its own right, *Explorations* counted among its more than eighty contributors both established and emerging scholars, scientists, and artists.

The think tank and the journal were supported by a grant from the Ford Foundation's newly established interdisciplinary research and study program in behavioral sciences (most likely cowritten by McLuhan and Carpenter and assisted by the then doctoral student Donald Theall). The group obtained $44,250 for a two-year research project devoted to studying the "changing patterns of language and behavior and the new media of communication."[2] Within North America, the Toronto group's proposal can be counted among the very first attempts to combine explicitly the study of culture *and* communication. The timing of this grant is significant given the scope of contemporaneous studies of media underway in the United States and Europe: functionalist and critical cultural studies of mass communications, theories of cybernetics, studies of social interaction, as well as psychological studies of the effects of media on human perception. Carpenter, initially the driving force behind *Explorations*, acted as editor of the first six issues before becoming coeditor with McLuhan for issues 7 and 8, which were sponsored by the *Toronto Telegram*. A ninth and final issue, entitled *Eskimo* (1959), combined Carpenter's writings on indigenous art and culture of the Aivilik juxtaposed with images from filmmaker Robert Flaherty and drawings by Frederick Varley. After Beacon Press published a selection of *Explorations* contributions in 1960, coedited by Carpenter and McLuhan as *Explorations in Communication*, McLuhan later resuscitated the spirit of *Explorations* as a "magazine within a magazine," a publication inside the University of Toronto's alumni magazine, the *Varsity Graduate* (1964–72).

2. *Ford Foundation, 1953, Ford Foundation Annual Report 1953*, New York: Ford Foundation: 67. The Ford Foundation's Behavioral Sciences Program had the stated goal of "improving the content of the behavioral sciences" by specifically supporting "interdisciplinary research and study." Launched in 1952, the program aimed to help the "intellectual development of the behavioral sciences" by "improving their relationship with such disciplines as history, social and political philosophy, humanistic studies and certain phases of economics" (67).

The group's proposal to Ford's Behavioral Sciences Program is revealing of the central assumptions that would underpin the graduate seminar and *Explorations*. The proposal's point of departure is not yet an assumption about the power of media forms to shape content, but rather the understanding that methods for studying new media required recognition of new patterns emerging across technological, cultural, and urban life. Underpinning the proposal is a conversation that McLuhan in particular had started with advocates of cybernetic theories. Carpenter was also of course conversant with the writings of anthropologists who were deeply involved with developing cybernetic models and metaphors within the social sciences, among others Gregory Bateson and Margaret Mead. Cybernetic theories also came to the group through Donald Theall, who would complete his PhD dissertation in 1954 on "Communication Theories in Modern Poetry: Yeats, Pound, Joyce and Eliot" under the supervision of both McLuhan and Carpenter.

"Well aware of the brilliant new developments in communication study at Massachusetts Institute of Technology," the Ford grant explains, gesturing both to Norbert Wiener's cybernetic conferences and to Claude Shannon and Warren Weaver's mathematical theory of communication, "the undersigned propose to utilize these insights but to employ also the technique of studying the forms of communication, old and new, as art forms," an approach already "implicit in the very title of Harold Innis' *Bias of Communication*."[3] The Toronto group proposed to study the effects of new media forms on patterns of language, economic values, social organization, individual and collective behaviour, always keeping in mind accompanying changes to the classroom and the networks of city life. In their eyes the central problem consisted of two aspects. First, "the creation of a new language of vision" that "arises from all our new visual media and which is part of the total language of modern culture." Second, the Toronto group proposed to study "the impact of this total social language on the traditional spoken and written forms of expression." These two core objectives they would pursue in the pages of *Explorations* through numerous contributions. As clearly indicated in an early draft of their Ford proposal, the core research group

3. Edmund S. Carpenter, Jaqueline Tyrwhitt, H. M. McLuhan, W. T. Easterbrook, and D. C. Williams, 1953, "University of Toronto: Changing Patterns of Language and Behavior and the New Media of Communication." Ford Foundation Archives. Grant File PA 53–70, Section 1, 1–11. Rockefeller Archive Center, New York: 4.

represented the five key disciplines that would supplement each other: anthropology, psychology, economics, town planning, and English.[4]

While no one discipline was privileged above the others, anthropology played a special role in creating a strong comparative framework from the start. In addition to anthropological discussions of cybernetics, the Sapir-Whorf theory was an important intellectual foundation. As with Innis, Edward Sapir (a German-born American who spent fifteen years in Ottawa working for the Geographical Survey of Canada) offered a multifocal habit of vision, working between linguistics, anthropology, and psychology. For the grant applicants, Sapir "brought together European attitudes towards psychoanalysis (emphasis on socially-situated personality) and North American attitudes towards social structure (culture)." Moreover, Sapir "fused the European concern with philology with [the] North American concern with dynamic patterns in language."[5] The anthropologist and ethnolinguist Dorothy Lee was arguably one of the group's "most influential force[s],"[6] contributing six articles on language, value, and perception. Her insight that peoples such as the Trobrianders perceived lineal order differently from Western cultures had already been cited by Bateson and Ruesch (1951), and was central to the delineation of acoustic and visual cultures undertaken by the Explorations group, and in later studies by both McLuhan and Carpenter.

In developing their methodologies, seminar faculty and graduate students undertook a number of critical media experiments on changing patterns of perception resulting from new media. The CBC and the then Ryerson Institute placed studio space and media equipment at their disposal. The experiment tested their central hypothesis that different media (speech, print, radio, television) lend themselves to different kinds of pedagogical experiences.[7] It is surprising that such findings have never been fully taken up by educational media researchers. Hopefully, the republication of these early studies will

4. "Changing Patterns of Man and Society Associated with the New Media of Communication." Draft of Ford Foundation Proposal, likely 1953. LAC MG 31, D 156, 204, 26.

5. Carpenter et al, 1953: 2.

6. Edmund Carpenter, 2001, "That Not-So-Silent Sea," in Donald F. Theall (Ed.), *The Virtual Marshall McLuhan* (p. 240), Montreal: McGill-Queen's University Press.

7. Edmund Carpenter, 1954, "Certain Media Biases," *Explorations* 3:65–74; Edmund Carpenter and Marshall McLuhan, 1956, "The New Languages," *Chicago Review* 10(1): 46–52; Edmund Carpenter, 1957, "The New Languages," *Explorations* 7:4–21.

renew interest in the cognitive studies of media which have focussed too narrowly, according to Carpenter and McLuhan, on attention and inputs and not enough on the creative and critical aspects of perception.

What is clear in reading through the *Explorations* issues is that Carpenter and McLuhan were most interested in the new kinds of learning made possible through the media. McLuhan, in particular, was influenced by research into human perception as part of his approach to media studies since he believed that these media were altering our senses, our forms of attention and knowledge production. Carpenter and McLuhan would assert that the media are transforming the human sensorium, an idea captured perhaps most playfully in the final coedited issue, *Explorations* 8, an ode to James Joyce devoted to the oral, to the new "acoustic space" of the electric age: "Verbi-Voco-Visual." The issue features seven essays, including one by McLuhan, that explore different aspects of oral culture—mostly concerned with a transition to a new orality. Twenty-four non-authored "Items," which include some previously published essays by McLuhan and Carpenter, appear as humorous intellectual sketches exploring topics like "Electronics as ESP," car commercials, bathroom acoustics, dictaphones, and of course wine. The final "Item," number 24, entitled "No Upside Down in Eskimo Art," reiterated McLuhan and Carpenter's core assertion that "after thousands of years of written processing of human experience, the instantaneous omnipresence of electronically processed information has hoicked us out of these age-old patterns into an auditory world." In the history of media studies in Canada and internationally, the *Explorations* journal is an important starting point for defining the rich new insights around new media cultures that the Toronto School helped inaugurate.

## References

Carpenter, Edmund S., Jaqueline Tyrwhitt, H. M. McLuhan, W. T. Easterbrook, and D. C. Williams. 1953. "University of Toronto: Changing Patterns of Language and Behavior and the New Media of Communication." Ford Foundation Archives. Grant File PA 53–70, Section 1, 1–11. Rockefeller Archive Center, New York.

Carpenter, Edmund. 1954. "Certain Media Biases." *Explorations* 3:65–74.

Carpenter, Edmund. 1957. "The New Languages." *Explorations* 7:4–21.

Carpenter, Edmund. 2001. "That Not-So-Silent Sea." In Donald F. Theall (Ed.), *The Virtual Marshall McLuhan* (pp. 236–61). Montreal: McGill-Queen's University Press.

Carpenter, Edmund, and Marshall McLuhan. 1956. "The New Languages." *Chicago Review* 10(1): 46–52.

Ford Foundation. 1953. *Ford Foundation Annual Report 1953*. New York: Ford Foundation.

Ruesch, Jurgen, and Gregory Bateson. 1951. *Communication, the Social Matrix of Psychiatry*. New York: Norton.

Theall, Donald. 1954. *Communication Theories in Modern Poetry: Yeats, Pound, Eliot and Joyce*. Doctoral dissertation. Toronto: University of Toronto.

# Summaries of All Eight
## *Explorations* Volumes

### Explorations 1

*Explorations* 1 took an audaciously new approach to communications and cultural research "cutting across" studies in anthropology, literature, social sciences, economics, folklore, and popular culture. From Copernican revolutions (Bidney) to a seventeenth-century translation of Sweden's Mohra witchcraft trials (Horneck); from senses of time (Leach) to the meaning of gongs (Carrington); from Majorcan customs (Graves) to a typography of functional analysis (Spiro); from Veblen's economic history (Riesman) to contemporary stress levels (Selye), the issue also included one of György Kepes's earliest drafts on fusing "art and science," an essay on Freud and vices (Goodman), and a return to childhood in Legman's work on comic books, before concluding with now classic essays by McLuhan and Frye. The cover of *Explorations* 1 depicts a series of masks from the award-winning film *The Loon's Necklace* (Crawley Films, 1948).

### Explorations 2

*Explorations* 2's mischievous spoof covers, both front and back, inside and outside, were labelled "Feenicht's Playhouse," a reference to the Phoenix playhouse of Joyce's *Wake*. The key playful headline, "New Media Changing Temporal and Spatial Orientation to Self," was accompanied by multiple hoax articles, including "Time-Space Duality Goes" and "TV Wollops MS," a reference to television's apparent power over manuscript culture as evidenced by the group's media experiment at CBC studios. Exemplifying the playfulness of the core faculty's discussions about new media and behaviour, it is not surprising the McLuhan would publish in this issue his now famous article "Notes on the Media as Art Forms" alongside essays by other seminar participants: Tyrwhitt resuscitated an unpublished article, "Ideal Cities and the City Ideal," a historical survey of proposals for ideal urban designs (originally drafted for the defunct journal *trans/formation: art, communication, environment*). Carpenter's "Eternal Life" is a first analysis of Aivilik Inuit concepts of time; then student Donald Theall's "Here Comes Everybody" offered a snapshot of his research on Joyce and communication theories in modern poetry; anthropologist Dorothy Lee, who would visit the seminar in March 1955, offered a review of David Bidney's challenge to scholarly traditions in his 1953 book *Theoretical Anthropology*. In addition, Carpenter fleshed out the contents with contributions from political economy, anthropology, psychology, and English: the second part of Riesman's Veblen study; Lord Raglan on social classes; Derek Savage on "Jung, Alchemy and Self"; the *New Yorker*'s Stanley Hyman on Malraux's thesis of the "museum without walls"; and A. Irving Hallowell's extended essay on "Self and its Behavioral Environment"—the inspiration for the spoof cover.

## Explorations 3

*Explorations* 3 was initially planned as a volume dedicated to Harold Innis. In the end, the issue would only include Innis's essay "Monopoly and Civilization," introduced by Easterbrook, and a series of reflections in "Innis and Communication" by seminar participants. In November 1954, the *Explorations* researchers attended the "Institute on Culture and Communication" organised by Ray Birdwhistell at the University of Louisville's Interdisciplinary Committee on Culture and Communication. A number of the contributions to *Explorations* 3 are essays or early drafts of contributions related to this conference (Birdwhistell, Lee, Trager & Hall). The issue also includes the initial, and substantially divergent, assessments of the group's first "media experiment" at CBC studios (April 1954) in the contributions by Carpenter and Williams. The issue is rounded out with an excerpt on reading and writing (Chaytor), a new translation of Kamo Chomei's *Hojoki* (Rowe & Kerrigan), a study of utopias (Wolfenstein), a reading of *Tristram Shandy* (MacLean), reflections on Soviet ethnography (Potekin & Levin), a reading of Shelley's hallucinations as narcissism and doublegoing (McCullough), a critical reassessment of the science of human behaviour (Wallace), and "Meat Packing and Processing," an anonymous entry, likely by McLuhan, alluding to Giedion's *Mechanization Takes Command* (1948). Like *Explorations* 1, the cover depicted an indigenous mask from the Northwest Coast also represented in the Crawley film *The Loon's Necklace* (1948).

## Explorations 4

According to McLuhan, *Explorations* 4 was planned as an issue devoted to Sigfried Giedion. Published in February 1955, with a cover adapted from Kandinsky's *Comets* (1938), *Explorations* 4 was devoted to issues of space and placed a strong emphasis on modes of linguistic and poetic thought across multiple media. Poems by e. e. cummings and Jorge Luis Borges mingle with essays by seminar leaders McLuhan on "Space, Time, and Poetry," Carpenter on "Eskimo Poetry: Word Magic," Tyrwhitt on "The Moving Eye" (regarding comparative perceptual experiences of Western cities and the ancient Indian city of Fatehpur Sikri), and Williams on "auditory space"—a notion that "electrified" the group, as Carpenter later recounted. Northrop Frye and Stephen Gilman's essays on poetic traditions were juxtaposed with Millar MacLure and Marjorie Adix's odes to Dylan Thomas, who had died in 1953. Case studies by then graduate students Walter J. Ong on "Space in Renaissance Symbolism" and Joan Rayfield on "Implications of English Grammar" were aligned with Dorothy Lee's contribution on "Freedom, Spontaneity and Limit in American Linguistic Usage" and Lawrence Frank's early draft of "Tactile Communication." Both Lee and Frank had presented their contributions at Ray Birdwhistell's "Institute on Culture and Communication" in Louisville, in 1954. A "Media Log" and the now famous entry "Five Sovereign Fingers Taxed the Breath," both largely replicated from McLuhan's 1954 *Counterblast* pamphlet, were published anonymously. In addition to "Our Enchanted Lives," a memorandum of instructions for television programming adapted from a Procter & Gamble memo, "The Party Line" offered a second alleged memorandum "To All TIME INC. Bureaus and Stringers." An "Idea File" containing insights on oral, written, and technological cultural forms was culled from writings by Robert Graves, Edmund Leach, Walter Gropius, and E. T. Hall, among many others. With *Explorations* 4, the group revealed its commitment to the belief that communication studies was deeply rooted in anthropological and literary-poetic traditions, but equally informed by studies of mechanisation, technology, and culture.

## Explorations 5

The cover of *Explorations* 5 returned to the playfulness of issue 2: the image of the famous Minoan "Our Lady of the Sports" figurine, held at the Royal Ontario Museum (the authenticity of which has long been disputed) was set in front of the *Toronto Daily Star*'s 8 April 1954 Home Edition front page, featuring the headline "H-Bomb in Mass Production, U.S." This juxtaposition between ancient artefact, contemporary media, and technological production set the stage for the issue: starting with Daisetz Suzuki's description of "Buddhist Symbolism", the issue follows with McLuhan's famous analysis of TV and radio in Joyce's *Finnegans Wake*. Such contrasts of new media forms continue with a "Portrait of James Joyce," an excerpt of a 1950 "Third Programme" BBC documentary edited by W. R. Rodgers, and the two-page "Anna Livia Plurabelle" section of Joyce's *Finnegans Wake*, set in experimental typography designed by Harley Parker and Toronto's Cooper and Beatty Ltd. The issue further juxtaposes essays by E. R. Leach on cultural conceptions of time and Jean Piaget on time-space conceptions of the child; anthropologists Claire Holt and Joan Rayfield on interpenetrations of language and culture and Carpenter's study of Eskimo space concepts; Rhodra Métraux on differences between the novel, play, and film versions of *The Caine Mutiny*; Roy Campbell on the fusion of oral and written traditions in the writings of Nigerian author Amos Tutuola, including an excerpt of his 1954 novel *My Life in the Bush of Ghosts*, and Harcourt Brown on Pascal; economist Kenneth Boulding on information theory and Easterbrook on economic approaches to communication; and an excerpt from Daniel Lerner and David Riesman's work on the modernisation of Turkey and the Middle East. Tyrwhitt and Williams contributed reflections on the seminar's second media experiment in "The City Unseen," an analysis of students' perceptions of the environment of the then Ryerson Institute. Anonymous entries included "Colour and Communication" and a transcription of satirist Jean Shepherd's radio broadcast "Channel Cat in the Middle Distance," likely courtesy of Carpenter. The issue is rounded out with a Letters File and an Ideas File, with contributions from E. R. Leach, Patrick Geddes, and Lawrence Frank.

## Explorations 6

Writing to the Explorations Group in 1954, Carpenter worried about the funds from the Ford grant that were available for publishing this issue. *Explorations* 6 was funded through the sales of issue 5 and possibly Carpenter's own funds. The cover image for this issue was a section of *The Great Wave*, by Katsushika Hokusai. According to Carpenter's letter, this issue summarizes the group's "ideas and findings," which though "not fully articulated" were "new and exciting." He saw the issue as "a full seminar statement." Indeed, the issue brings together the interdisciplinary reflections and comparative media studies that characterized the group's methodology: a brilliant essay by radical anthropologist Dorothy Lee on "Wintu thought" (Lee would ultimately publish six essays in *Explorations* and had a significant influence on the seminar) and two essays on television that were solicited to reflect upon different geographical differences that shaped the experiences of the new medium—one in the US (Chayefsky) and the other the Soviet Union (Sharoyeva, the "top man" in the USSR television system). Also included were Giedion's classic essay on cave painting; a reflection on the phonograph alongside a consideration of "print's monopoly" by C. S. Lewis; as well as essays by McLuhan on media and events; language and magic (Maritain); writing and orality (Riesman); color (Parker); the evolution of the human mind (Montagu); and the anonymous entries "Print's Monopoly" and "Feet of Clay," likely drafted by McLuhan and Carpenter, which take up conflicts between old and new media environments. This issue contains the full spectrum of the weekly seminar's research undertakings over a two-year period.

## Explorations 7

*Explorations* 7 (1957), the only issue without a table of contents, was edited by Carpenter and McLuhan solely and, with issue 8, sponsored by the *Toronto Telegram*. Easterbrook and Tyrwhitt were away, and Williams wanted his name taken off the masthead, allegedly because of the publication of American writer Gershon Legman's infamous "Bawdy Song . . . in Fact and in Print," a history of erotic writing. McLuhan had contributed to Legman's short-lived but hugely influential magazine *Neurotica* (1948–52), so the two had a previous connection. But the tension between Williams and the editors might have also been due to their different interpretations of the CBC/Ryerson media experiments which explored media sensory biases with a group of students discussed in issue 3 by Williams in scientific terms, and here again by Carpenter in his essay "The New Languages" in cultural terms. Carpenter argues that each medium (radio, TV, print) "codifies reality differently." To accompany this opening essay, they each included anonymous entries: the essay "Classroom Without Walls," later attributed to McLuhan, explores the ubiquitous mediasphere outside educational institutions, which teachers must begin to consider as an inherent and unavoidable pedagogical experience, followed by "Songs of the Pogo," a reference to the popular comic and LP of the period, which pervaded the McLuhan home. McLuhan saw relationships between "Jazz and Modern Letters," juxtaposed with Carpenter's reflections on the acoustic character of ancient and preliterate symbols, masks, and traditions in "Eternal Life of the Dream." Dorothy Lee contributed two essays to the issue on lineal and non-lineal codifications examined in the Trobriand language with responses by Robert Graves. The focus on educational matters also included a review of Riesman's *Variety and Constraint in American Education* as well as examinations of the cultural specificity of the Soviet press, Soviet novels, and Soviet responses to Elvis Presley. The particularity of an oral and noncapitalistic culture had been an important point of comparison for the Explorations Group, especially Carpenter and McLuhan. Harley Parker designed the issue's cover.

## *Explorations* 8

*Explorations* 8 (1957) is perhaps the most famous of all the issues. It was devoted to the oral—"Verbi-Voco-Visual"—and was edited primarily by McLuhan and again published by the *Toronto Telegram* and the University of Toronto. The issue was filled with visual experimentation; framed by extensive play with typography in the spirit of the Vorticists and for the first time the extensive use of "flexitype" by Harley Parker, then display designer at the ROM. Seen throughout are Parker's experiments with typography as well as color printing, the first time in the history of the journal. A photomontage from László Moholy-Nagy's *Vision in Motion* (1947) depicting a man's face with an ear juxtaposed over an eye is the frontispiece to the issue. The issue features seven essays, including one by McLuhan, that explore different aspects of oral culture—mostly concerned with a transition to a new orality. Twenty-four non-authored "Items," which include some previously published essays by McLuhan and Carpenter, appear as humorous intellectual sketches exploring topics like "Electronics as ESP," car commercials, bathroom acoustics, dictaphones, and of course wine. The final "Item," number 24, entitled "No Upside Down in Eskimo Art," reiterated McLuhan and Carpenter's core assertion that "after thousands of years of written processing of human experience, the instantaneous omnipresence of electronically processed information has hoicked us out of these age-old patterns into an auditory world."

**Michael Darroch** (University of Windsor)
**Janine Marchessault** (York University)
2016

# VOLUME 3

In the medieval world, those who could read or write were the few, and it is likely that most of them did not read or write with our methods or with our facility. In order to gain some idea of the difficulties under which they laboured, it is necessary to consider what mental processes are involved in the understanding of spoken or written speech. Psychologists are by no means agreed upon this subject, but most of them would probably accept the following account of its implications.

When we hear the phrase, 'give me that book', the word 'book' is recognised as a familiar collocation of sounds; in psychological language, we gain an 'acoustic image' which experience enables us to identify. This experience includes not only the recognition of particular sounds, but also takes into account pitch, emphasis and intonation; the individual word 'book', spoken in isolation, would evoke an image, but would convey no information stimulating to action, unless such information were provided by gesture or emphasis or intonation. In some languages the isolated word has different meanings, according to the 'tone' used by the speaker. All languages are, to some extent, 'tone' languages; the simple phrase, 'Good morning', may mean, according to the manner of its utterance, 'I'm delighted to see you', or, 'Here's that infernal bore again'; it may mean, 'Thank goodness, he's going', or 'Come again when you can'.

Experience, therefore, takes into account other matters than the sounds which compose an individual word; but for the purpose of this analysis, we confine our attention to the word as such. The acoustic image may be translated into the visual image of a book, and if the hearer is illiterate, this is probably the end of the process. If the hearer can read, he will substitute for the visual image of a book the printed word 'book', and in either case there may be a half-felt tendency to articulate the word, a feeling known to psychology as a 'kinesthetic' or 'speech-motor' image.

When, therefore, a child is learning to read, his task is to construct from printed symbols an acoustic image which he can recognise. When recognition has been achieved, he pronounces the word, not only for the satisfaction of his teacher, but also because he cannot himself understand the printed symbols without transforming them into sounds; he can read only aloud. When he can read faster than he can speak, pronunciation becomes a rapid muttering, and eventually ceases entirely. When this stage has been reached, the child has substituted a visual for an acoustic image, and so long as he continues to be dependent upon printed matter, as most of us are, this condition is never likely to change. When we read, the visual image of the printed word-form instantaneously becomes an acoustic image; kinesthetic images accompany it, and if we are not reading aloud, the combination of the two produces 'inner speech', which, in the case of most people, includes both inner speaking and inner hearing. It may be that inner pronunciation falls below the threshold of consciousness in the case of those greatly occupied with printed matter; but it will rise to the surface, if the individual begins to read a foreign language in a script with which he is not entirely familiar, or to learn by heart a difficult passage which must be orally reproduced verbatim. It is said that some doctors forbid patients with severe throat afflictions to read, because silent reading provokes motions of the vocal organs, though the reader may not be conscious of them. So also when we speak or write, ideas evoke acoustic combined with kinesthetic images, which are at once transformed into visual word images. The speaker or writer can now hardly conceive of language, except in printed or written forms; the reflex actions by which the process of reading or writing is performed have become so 'instinctive' and are performed with such facile rapidity, that the change from the auditory to the visual is concealed from the reader or writer, and makes analysis of it a matter of great difficulty. It may be that acoustic and kinesthetic images are inseparable, and that 'image' as such is an abstraction made for purposes of analysis, but which is non-existent considered in itself and as pure. But whatever account the individual may render of his own mental processes, and most of us are far from competent in this respect, the fact remains that his idea of language is irrevocably modified by his experience of printed matter.

The result is that we cannot think of language without reference to its written or printed form, and many prefer the printed to the written word, because print is clearer to them; it relieves a strain upon the memory and gives time for deliberate consideration. The hearer to whom a letter has been read will ask to see the script, in order to make sure that he has missed no point; he will take notes of a lecture, lest he should forget matters of interest; no policeman is complete without a pencil to lick and a notebook wherein to scrawl. Visualisation can even be an aid to memory; most of us have a clear image, even in advanced age, of certain pages in our first Latin grammar or our first repetition book, and educational writers have begun to realise that the 'lay-out' of the page is almost as important to the learner as the matter which it contains. It is by visual practice that we master the vagaries of English orthography, and so-called bad spellers are often those who are misled by inability to exclude auditory reminiscences; they may be seen, when in doubt, to write down a word on scribbling paper, 'to see how it looks', to recover, that is, a visual memory which has become blurred. Hearing and sight once disconnected, have become inseparable; when we hear a speaker, the effect of his words is transmitted from the auditory to the visualising capacity, and we see, or can see, the words 'in our mind's eye', whether we wish to take notes or not. And when we read to ourselves, the visual impression is accompanied by an auditory perception; we hear, or can hear, the sentences that we read, and when we compose, we write to the dictation of an inner voice.

Sound and sight, speech and print, eye and ear have nothing in common. The human brain has done nothing that compares in complexity with this fusion of ideas involved in linking up the two forms of language. But the result of the fusion is that once it is achieved in our early years, we are for ever after unable to think clearly, independently and surely about any one aspect of the matter. We cannot think of sounds without thinking of letters; we believe letters have sounds. We think that the printed page is a picture of what we say, and that the mysterious thing called 'spelling' is sacred. . . . The invention of printing broadcast the printed language and gave to print a degree of authority that it has never lost.[1]

---

[1] A. Lloyd James, *Our Spoken Language*, London, 1938, p. 29.

Children can learn languages more easily than adults, because they can concentrate wholly upon audition and are not hampered by habits of visualisation; just for that reason, they forget almost as rapidly as they learn, unless they are in continual contact with the language concerned. For the adult to return to the infantile stage of simple auditory perception is a task of extraordinary difficulty for those who are obliged to face it, as, for instance, the missionary who proposes to reduce an unwritten language to writing. He must first learn it as a spoken tongue until he is so fully master of it as to be able to decompose the words he has heard into their component sounds and find a symbol to represent each sound, in fact, to form an alphabet. But in this task, he will be continually hampered by the fact that he has been accustomed to regard language as visualised in the garb of a written orthography.

But when the ordinary well-educated man is learning a new language and hears an unfamiliar word, supposing him to have reached the stage of ability to separate the words of a new language, his instinctive inquiry is how is it spelt? what does it look like in writing? from what is it derived or with what known words is it cognate? Given this help, he can associate the new acquisition with his previous experience and has a chance of making a permanent addition to his vocabulary. But if he has to depend upon audition alone, he will certainly forget the new word, unless circumstances oblige him to make use of it forthwith and frequently. Such is the consequence of association with print; in printer's ink auditory memory has been drowned and visual memory has been encouraged and strengthened.

Thought, in the full sense of the term, is hardly possible without words. When ideas arise above the threshold of consciousness, they are formulated by the mind in words; accustomed as we are to import and receive information by means of language, we inevitably follow the same method when we are occupied by mental consideration; we discuss a matter with ourselves as we might discuss it with an interlocutor, and such discussion cannot be conducted without the use of words. Hence, until ideas can be formulated in words, they can hardly be regarded as fully conceived. Here, an objection is raised: unless the thinker possesses words, he cannot think; but, unless he has thought, he cannot possess words, how then was the process begun? Did ideas precede language, or is capacity for speech innate and awaiting only the stimulus of ideas provoked by external accident, in order to break into action? In other words, did the hen or the egg come first? This question has interested those concerned with the origins of language, but it does not affect the reality of inner speech as the method of inner thought. This reality has been admitted from the days of Homer to our own time. Odysseus alone upon his raft and confronted by the rising storm, 'in trouble spake to his own great soul' for some twenty hexameter lines; and a public-house orator, describing his domestic troubles, will say: 'then I sez to meself, this 'ere 'as got ter stop', and will conclude his catastrophic narrative, 'so I sez to meself, I must 'ave a pint and I comes rahnd 'ere'. If the thinker is illiterate, the images that arise in his mind will be auditory; if he is literate, they will be visual; in either case, immediate vocal expression can be given to them, if necessary.

As has been said, this vocal expression is necessary to children who are learning to read or to inexperienced adults; they cannot understand the written or printed symbols without transforming them into audible sounds. Silent reading comes with practice, and when practice has made perfect, we do not realise the extent to which the human eye has adapted itself to meet our requirements. If we take a line of printed matter, cut it lengthways in half, so that the upper half of the lettering is exactly divided from the lower half, and then hand the slips to two friends, we shall probably find that the man with the upper half will read the line more easily than the man with the lower half. The eye of the practised reader does not take the whole of the lettering, but merely so much as will suggest the remainder to his experienced intelligence. Similarly, if we listen to a speaker with a difficult delivery, we instinctively supply syllables and even words which we have failed to hear. Nor does the eye halt at each separate word. When we read our own language, we halt at a point in the line, notice a few letters on either side of it, and proceed to another halting point; the eye has not seen the whole formation of every word, but has seen enough to infer the meaning of the passage. Hence the difficulty of proof-reading; our usual method of reading allows us to pass over misprints, because we see enough of any one word to take its correctness for granted. The number of these halting places will vary with the nature of the matter to be read; in a foreign language they will be more numerous than when we are concerned with our own familiar tongue, and if we are reading a manuscript in a crabbed hand with many contractions, we shall be forced to proceed almost letter by letter.

Very different was the case of the medieval reader. Of the few who could read, few were habitual readers; in any case the ordinary man of our own times probably sees more printed and written matter in a week than the medieval scholar saw in a year. Nothing is more alien to medievalism than the modern reader, skimming the headlines of a newspaper and glancing down its columns to glean any point of interest, racing through the pages of some dissertation to discover whether it is worth his more careful consideration, and pausing to gather the argument of a page in a few swift glances. Nor is anything more alien to modernity than the capacious medieval memory which, untrammelled by the associations of print, could learn a strange language with ease and by the methods of a child, and could retain in memory and reproduce lengthy epic and elaborate lyric poems. Two points, therefore, must be emphasised at the outset. The medieval reader, with few exceptions, did not read as we do; he was in the stage of our muttering childhood learner; each word was for him a separate entity and at times a problem, which he whispered to himself when he had found the solution; this fact is a matter of interest to those who edit the writings which he reproduced.[1] Further, as readers were few and hearers numerous, literature in its early days was produced very largely for public recitation; hence, it was rhetorical rather than literary in character, and rules of rhetoric governed its composition.

Even a superficial acquaintance with medieval literature will show that its exponents continued the custom of public recitation common in classical times. The complaint of Juvenal's opening satire may well have been repeated in medieval times. Authors read their works in public, as this was the only way in which they could publish them; Giraldus Cambrensis read his *Topographia Hiberniae* before a public meeting at Oxford for three days in succession to different audiences. Private readings to a circle of friends were more common than these set performances, and naturally increased as manuscripts were multiplied and education spread. It was a public perhaps more eager to hear stories than to gather information that supported the numerous professional story-tellers, the ministrels and jongleurs who went about the countries and were as necessary to medieval society as was their counterpart in Arab civilisation. They performed the business of providing amusement which has been taken over by the radio and the cinema at the present time. Authors expressly state that their work is intended to be recited; a glance at such a work as *Les Incipit des Poèmes français antérieurs au XVIe Siècle* (A. Langfors, Paris, 1917) will provide numerous statements and exhortations of this kind. 'Or oez tuit coumunement', 'Or oiez un flabel courtois', 'Or escoutez, grans et menour', 'Or entendez tuit par amor', are almost conventional exordia.

---

[1] Under the rule of St. Benedict, each monk was to receive a book from the library: 'accipiant omnes singulos codices de bibliotheca, quos per ordinem ex integra legant; qui codices in caput Quadragesimae dandi sunt' (Regula, cap. xlviii). No limit of time was set and the books appear to have been returned at the beginning of the succeeding Lent. A year for one book seems a generous allowance; but the slowness of the medieval reader *is* obvious from this instance.

The introduction of conversations provided opportunities for personification and dramatic delivery; asseverations of the truth of the tale, reinforced by appeals to heaven, were intended to enlist the interest of the audience, which is encouraged to visualise exciting scenes by the use of 'epideictic' expressions: 'Es vos un angle qui descent de la nue'; 'La veissies un estor esbaudir'. These points alone clearly show that such compositions were not written to be read à la Macaulay, 'with your feet upon the fender'. The whole technique of *chanson de geste, roman d'adventure,* and lyric poem presupposed, as will be seen, a hearing, not a reading public. When culture had reached that stage at which the individual read to himself for his own enjoyment, a different kind of literature was in demand.

The habits of the medieval reader or scribe are well illustrated by a passage in Grimmelshausen's *Simplicissimus* (Book 1, chap. 10); the hero informs us: 'als ich das erstemal den Einsiedel in der Bibel lesen sahe, konnte ich mir nicht einbilden, mit wem er doch ein solch heimlich und meinem Bedünken nach sehr ernstlich Gespräch haben müsste. Ich sahe wohl die Bewegung seiner Lippen, hörte auch das Gebrummel, hingegen aber sahe und hörte ich niemand, der mit ihm redete.' The passage recalls the situation in Acts viii. 30, where Philip hears the eunuch of Candace reading Isaiah with no visible audience. When we encounter anyone poring over a newspaper, and whispering the words to himself as he laboriously spells his way through the sheet, we set him down as uneducated. It is not commonly realised that this was the manner of reading generally practised in the ancient world and during the early days of Christianity. For these periods the case has been fairly well proved by Joseph Balogh, who develops the statements made by Eduard Norden (*Die antike Kunstprosa,* Leipsig, 1898); but Balogh provides very little evidence for the medieval period, and draws most of his evidence from patristic literature. This ancient practice was continued in medieval times, until it was killed by the dissemination of printed matter, and the habit of mind which it implies deserves the notice of those who take in hand the editing of medieval texts.

Professor Vinaver contributed to the *Studies Presented to M. K. Pope* an article upon textual emendation in which he analysed the mental processes incident to the copying of a manuscript, and showed with much penetration how such mistakes as those classified under the names 'homoioteleuton', 'dittography' and similar aberrations can occur. But this ingenious analysis and the diagrams which illustrate it seem to labour under one defect; they assume that the medieval scribe adopted

7

exactly the mental attitude that one of ourselves would assume if he were occupied in copying a manuscript for his own purposes. This was certainly not the case, for the reason that we gain the majority of our information and the ideas from printed matter, whereas the medieval obtained them orally. He was confronted not by the beautiful productions of a university press, but by a manuscript often crabbed in script and full of contractions, and his instinctive question, when deciphering a text, was not whether he had seen, but whether he had heard this or that word before; he brought not a visual but an auditory memory to his task. Such was the result of his upbringing; he had learnt to rely on the memory of spoken sounds, not upon the interpretation of written signs. And when he had deciphered a word he pronounced it audibly.[1]

If the evidence for this habit of mind and action seems scanty, it must be remembered that early testimony is constantly silent upon subjects concerning which we should like to have information, simply because these matters were so universally common as to pass without comment. As evidence falling within medieval times may be quoted the *Rule of St. Benedict,* chap. xlviii, which ordered the monks 'post sextam (horam) surgentes a mensa, pausent in lecta sua cum omni silentio; aut forte qui voluerit legere, sibi sic legat ut alium non inquietet', which suggests that the common manner of reading to oneself meant whispering or muttering. Bernard Pez relates of Richalm of Schönthal: 'oftentimes, when I am reading straight from the book and in thought only, as I am wont, they (devils) make me read aloud by word, that they may deprive me so much the more of the inward understanding thereof, and that I may the less penetrate into the interior force of the reading, the more I pour myself out in exterior speech'. This is the case of a man who is trying to accustom himself to silent reading and has not yet formed the habit. Johannes Busch, a great monastic reformer (1450), received a reply to a letter: 'Predilecte pater Johannes in Windesem! Litera vestra dulciter sonuit in auribus meis.' So Erasmus wrote to the Hungarian Bishop Nicolaus Oláh in 1533: 'Oro ut hanc epistolam legas solus nec huic tabellioni quicquam arcani committas'; the reading of a private letter by the recipient might be overheard. The following is an obvious case of one who reads aloud to himself:

---

[1] The process is thus described by a copyist of the eighth century on concluding his work: 'qui scribere nescit nullum putat esse laborem. Tres digiti scribunt, duo oculi vident. Una lingua loquitur, totum corpus laborat, et omnis labor, finem habet, et praemium ejus non habet finem' (Wattenbach, *Schriftwesen im Mittelalter,* Leipzig, 1896, p. 495). Three fingers hold the pen, the eyes see the words, the tongue pronounces them as they are written and the body is cramped with leaning over a desk. The scribe is obviously unable to avoid the necessity of pronouncing each word as he deciphers it.

An ek in other wise also
Ful ofte time it falleth so,
Min Ere with a good pitaunce
Is fedd of redinge of romaunce
Of Ydoine and of Amadas,
That whilom weren in mi cas,
And eke of othere mony a score,
That loveden longe er I was bore,
For whan I of here loves rede,
Min Ere with the tale I fede.

There were undoubtedly cases of silent reading; the well-known instance of Ambrosius described by St. Augustine (*Confessions*, Book vi, chap. 3) is perhaps repeated in Chaucer (*The Hous of Fame*, II, 148):

Thou goost hoom to the hous anoon,
And, also domb as any stoon,
Thou sittest at another boke,
Til fully daswed is thy loke.

Thomas Hoccleve, who spent most of his life as a writer in the Privy Seal Office, defended his occupation against those who thought writing an easy occupation as compared with manual labour, in his translation of the *De Regimine Principum*, which he made in 1411–12.

A writer mot thre thynges to hym knytte,
And in those may be no disseverance;
Mynde, ee and hand, non may fro othir flitte,
    But in them mot be joint contynuance.
    The mynd, al hoole withouten variance,
        On the ee and hand awayte mot alway,
        And thei two eek on hym; it is no nay.

Whoso schal wryte, may nat holde a tale
With hym and hym, ne synge this ne that;
But alle his wittes grete and smale
    Thor must apperc, and halden them therat,
    And syn he speke may, ne synge nat,
        But bothe two he needes moot forbere:
        His labour to hym is the alengere.

Hoccleve, as a professional writer, had probably learnt the habit of silent reading. The hired *scriptor* or scrivener began to supplement or to replace the monastic scribe at an early date; St. Albans made regu-

9

lations for the employment of such professionals before the middle of the thirteenth century; in the late fourteenth century the York scriveners formed a guild of their own. In university towns the scrivener could make a steady income; those who were under university control were occupied with books on law, theology or medicine, and authors of *belles-lettres* had to content themselves with scriveners not thus occupied, who were less reliable than the more professional class.

But such practised readers were regarded as exceptional. Further evidence may be seen in the strict rule of silence in the medieval scriptorium. Alcuin wished to protect the copyists of religious texts in the scriptorium at Tours from any distraction of the kind:

> Hic sedeant sacrae scribentes famina legis,
>   Nec non sanctorum dicta sacrata patrum;
> His interserere caveant sua frivola verbis,
>   Frivola ne propter erret et ipsa manus.
> Correctosque sibi quaerant studiose libellos,
>   Tramite quo recto penna volantis eat.
> Per cola distinguant proprios et commata sensus,
>   Et punctos ponant ordine quosque suo,
> Ne vel falsa legat taceat vel forte repente
>   Ante pios fratres lector in ecclesia.

This caution may be directed against idle chatter; but murmuring and whispering would be equally objectionable. Dictation was probably but little employed in monasteries as a means of multiplying copies of manuscripts and where not more than one copy at a time was expected, silence was the rule. At Tournai in the twelfth century, the Abbé Odo had books copied, 'ita ut si claustrum ingredereris, videres plerumque xii monarchos juvenes in cathedris sedentes et super tabulas diligenter et artificiose compositas cum silentio scribentes'. The arrangement of certain monastic libraries suggest the same purpose. Part of the cloister was often used for reading and perhaps writing, and was divided into niches or stalls, each to contain a monk and his book. In the Rites of Durham (Surtees Society, vol. CVII (1902), p. 83) a description of this arrangement is given: 'in the north syde of the Cloister from the corner over against the Church Dour to the corner over againste the Dorter dour was all fynely glased from the hight to the sole within a little of the grownd into the Cloyster garth, and in every wyndowe iii pewes or Carrells where every one of the old monkes has his Carrell severall by himselfe, that when they had dyned they dyd resorte to that place of Cloister, and there studyed upon there bookes, every one in his Carrell all the after none unto evensong tyme; this was there Exercise every daie; all there pewes or Carrells was all fynely wainscotted, and verie close all but the fore part which had carved wourke that gave light in at ther carrell doures of wainscott; and in every Carrell was a deske to lye there bookes on; and the Carrells was no greater then from one stanchell of the wyndowe to another'. A similar arrangement was in force in the cloister of Gloucester Abbey. Why this attempt to secure privacy in establishments where the inmates as a rule spent most of their time among their fellows? For the same reason that the reading-room of the British Museum is not divided into sound-proof compartments. The habit of silent reading has made such an arrangement unnecessary; but fill the reading room with medieval readers and the buzz of whispering and muttering would be intolerable.

These facts deserve greater attention from the editors of medieval texts. When the eye of a modern copyist leaves the manuscript before him in order to write, he carries in his mind a visual reminiscence of what he has seen. What the medieval scribe carried was an auditory memory, and probably in many cases, a memory of one word at a time. Zauner[1] has suggested that this habit has had an influence upon the development of final consonants: 'man wird wohl in Afrz. gesprochen haben: *il est arrivez,* aber, *il es morz* (wie etwa *aestimare* nicht *estmer,* sondern *esmer* geworden war), *tot arme,* aber *to muet.* Dass die Schrift davon so gut wie nichts weiss, erklärt sich wohl dadurch, dass die mittelalterlichen Schreiber während des Schreibens die Wörter vor sich hinflüsterten, also wirklich isoliert sprachen.' To this cause may be attributed some of the inconsistencies in the orthography of scribes, which were not necessarily due to mere carelessness; if a scribe was copying a text composed in a dialect not native to himself, he was likely to substitute his own auditory memory of the text for his visual impression of it, and to write *er* instead of *ar, el* for *al* and the like. Paul Meyer's remarks upon the scribe of the unique manuscript of *Guillaume le Maréchal* (*Société de l'Histoire de France,* Paris, 1891, III, pp. cxxxvi ff.) shows that he was an Englishman imposing his own orthography upon a French original which he was copying, and several of his deformations of place and proper names with which he was not familiar are due to his reliance upon auditory memory.

To the same tendency may be due the rimes in Beroul's *Tristran* (ed. A. Ewart, Blackwell, 1940), *voier: soir,* 1.473; *choier; doloir,* 1.3937, where the scribe has substituted his own pronounciation for the correct rime in *-oir.* It must also be remembered that the individual cannot

---

[1] *Leuvensche Bijdragen* XV, 1923, III, pp. 77 ff.

criticise the correctness of his own pronunciation; mimetic capacity varies greatly in individuals and the speaker is himself no judge of his success or failure in imitating the sounds he hears. A German immigrant to America will pronounce 'dollar' as 'dahler' on the analogy of 'thaler' and remain sublimely unconscious that his pronunciation is incorrect; he identifies a mistaken auditory memory of the word with a correct visual memory of it. It is also possible for the two memories to become confused, when a word will be spelt differently, even when it recurs in close succession.

Instances in which the difference between auditory and visual memory can be made a basis for emendation will naturally vary in frequency with the education and competence of the scribe. On the whole, the orthography of French texts in the twelfth and thirteenth centuries is surprisingly uniform and suggests an elaboration of rules and a training of scribes more extensive than might have been expected at so early a period. But training and experience varied in different cases. Editors of texts have to estimate the competence of any scribe with whose work they have to deal; such cases cannot be subjected to fixed rules and scribes have to be considered as individuals, and it is not waste of time to consider the psychological reasons for their mistakes and aberrations.

*H. J. Chaytor*

# I

The waters of the river move on and on. And the waters are never the same. The bubbles of the whirlpool break, and form again, and disappear again. And so it is in this world with man and his dwellings.

In the pearl-like cities, the houses lie so close one to the other that their tiled roofs seem locked in combat. A man's dwelling is commonly thought to survive him through the generations; but is this really true? How often do we remark a truly ancient house? Those we see either replace others which are devastated or they are once-great houses which have been broken up. And so with the men who dwell in them: they fall away and are gone. A man dies in the morning to be reborn in the shadow of night. Born in ignorance to die in ignorance, he lives unknowing—not knowing even for whom in this world his heart bears so much pain, not knowing even by what means to find his pleasure. Man and his house are rivals in impermanence. They are like the dew on the face of the morning glory: the dew vanishes and the flower stays to fade in the morning sun, or the flower fades and the dew stays, only to be gone before evening.

I remember the terrible disaster in the third year of the era of Angen.[1] It was the twenty-eighth day of the fourth month. The wind was howling fiercely and would not quiet down. At dusk, the hour of the Dog, fire broke out in the Dragon quarter of the city and raged its way to the quarter of the Wild Boar. It spread as far as the Red Sparrow Gate. In a single night all was reduced to rubble and ashes. It was said that the blaze began in the Lane of the Sluice, in a house which was being temporarily used to house the sick of the city. The restless winds drove the flames one way and then another, and they spread like the fingers of a fan. In the houses farthest from the flames people were suffocated by the smoke. The houses within reach of its fury were engulfed. Ashes swirled up to the sky, and heaven and earth glowed red. Flames breaking from the wind seemed to leap whole city blocks. In the midst of all this horror what man could remain in his right mind? Some fell to the ground smothered by the smoke, others ran crazily confused straight into the devouring flames, to die in an instant. Even those who escaped with their skins did not manage to save their wealth. At last only embers and rubble remained. Many thousands of persons died, and the number of horses and cattle lost was incalculable.

In all the preposterousness of his ways man commits no greater folly than to spend his wealth building his home in peril-filled cities.

I remember, too, the disaster of the fourth year of the era of Jisho.[2] On the twenty-ninth day of the month of the Hare, a terrifying tornado rose up in the quarter of the Great Central Gate. It raced across the city, howling through an area of three or four wards. Of all the houses in its path, mansions and huts alike, not one escaped damage. Either they were flattened completely or only the framework was left standing. The roofs of gates were snatched off by the gale and carried four and five blocks away. Fences were blown to the ground—so that every man's yard was made one with his neighbour's. The contents of the houses rose in a mad dance to the skies and the shingles of the roofs were like winter leaves scattering before the wind. Dust towered up like clouds of smoke to hide the sky, blinding men's eyes. Not a word could be heard over the shrieking of the gale. Even the wailing winds of hell could not compare. The destruction of homes was not the worst of the disaster, for the number of men injured and crippled while trying to save their dwellings was beyond count. At last, the wind moved off toward the Goat and Ape quarter of the city.

Any tempest is a fearful thing, but this was indeed no ordinary wind. It was thought to be a portent of even greater evil to come.

---

[1] 1175 A.D.
[2] 1180 A.D.

Again, in the waterless month of the same year, it was decided to move the capital. The decision came as a complete surprise to the people: this place had been the site of the capital for several centuries, ever since its selection by the Emperor Saga. No reason for the change was given. Because the move was not easy, the populace was discontented and complained as never before. But their murmuring availed nothing. And eventually the entire court, beginning with the Emperor, moved to the new site. The populace followed. For what man who cared for his place in the world could consent to remain in an empty city? Every man who valued rank or station or who curried favour vied with his rival to leave. Only those who were out of step with the world or whom the world had rejected and who held no further hope for the future stayed behind in their melancholy after the others had gone.

The houses which had competed with each other in ostentation were torn down. The structures were taken apart and floated down the Yodo River to the new capital; and the land returned to weeds under men's eyes. And men's hearts changed. Only the saddled horse was valued and men no longer used the stately bullock-drawn carriage. Only the fief land in the south and west, the region nearest the new capital, was sought after, while the lands in the north and east, farthest away, were scorned. After some while I had occasion to visit the new capital, and I could see for myself that the site was far too small to accommodate a city. It was too small to lay out streets suitable for a capital. To the north were towering mountains, and to the south the land fell away to the sea. The crashing of the waves unceasingly assailed one's ears and the salt winds blew with unabating fierceness. The Imperial Palace itself was lost to view in the mountain fastness. It was so oddly crude that one wondered if the Tree-Bark palace of the Emperor Tenji,[1] so long ago, had not been like this. Still, it was not without a certain grace and elegance.

Every day more houses were pulled down in the old capital and the waters of the Yodo were choked with timbers floating downstream to the new city. The old capital was already grown over with weeds even before the new was finished. Men were as restless and unquiet as the floating clouds. The old landholders at the new site were discomposed by the loss of their lands, while the newcomers were vexed at having to build once more. At length, the graceful ways of the Court disappeared

---

[1] *The Tree-Bark Palace* (Ki No Maru Den 木の丸殿 )

The Emperor Tenji, in testimony of his grief for the death of his mother, ordered a palace to be constructed of trees from which the bark had not been removed. Later emperors imitated the custom as a symbol of humility and frugality.

15

and men behaved like louts or country samurai.[1] There were those who asked if all this were not perhaps an omen to presage even greater chaos. And events proved them correct. As the days passed, the confusion became greater and men grew disquieted. Disorder was culminated finally when in the winter of the same year the Court announced a return to the former capital.

And what of the houses which had been torn down? I know not. But they were never restored.

We are told that in ancient times our sovereigns ruled the land with true wisdom and beneficence. The roof of the Imperial Palace was of bare thatch, and the rough edges of the eaves were left untrimmed. When it was noticed by the rulers that the smoke rose thinly from the chimneys of the people's houses, all levies and tributes were excused. —But this was long ago.

## II

Then I remember the disaster which began in the era of Yowa.[2] For two years the land was ravaged by drought and famine. In the spring and summer there was drought, and in the fall and winter, wind and flood completed the devastation. Not one of the five grains had a chance to ripen. In the spring, it was futile to till the land for the summer's planting—as men had always done. There was no bustle at harvest-time and no food was stored for the winter. In desperation people began to abandon their land and move away. Some even fled to the hills. All forms of prayer were offered up and extraordinary rites invoked, but nothing availed. City people must depend upon the country, but now there was no one in the country to supply their needs. The pride of the city dwellers forced them to keep up appearances as long as possible, and day and night they offered prayers. They tried to sell their valuables at prices so absurd it seemed they wanted only to be rid of them. But no one would even look at their wares. Those who would buy offered only money—which no one wanted—and never so much as a cup-full of the coveted grain. The roads were everywhere lined with beggars, and their wailing filled the air. For a year this went on, everyone believing that the next year would be better than the last. But these hopes were crushed by the plague which came with the following year. Things grew

---

[1] *Samurai*

Until the Restoration, a member of the military class, warrior, man-of-arms. The Samurai received a pension from their Daimyo and owed him absolute allegiance. The code of Bushido prescribed unwavering and inflexible loyalty to a lord and self-destruction to atone for failure. The tale of the forty-seven Ronin who committed hara-kiri in a body in atonement for the death of their master is known to every Japanese school boy. The Samurai's nearest equivalent in the West was the medieval knight, but contrary to the chivalric code, the ethics of Bushido are unconcerned with allegiance to women or to any religious principle.
[2] 1181 A.D.

16

more horrible, until it seemed the whole world must die of starvation. As the situation went from bad to worse, the scene was reminiscent of the fable in which the fishes floundered in the dried-up pool. Matters came to such a pass that even men of high station, men whose feet were covered and who could afford hats, humbly went about from house to house begging for food. People grew senile and feeble in their suffering, and, even as one watched—wondering how they managed to stay on their feet—they would topple and die before one's eyes. The corpses piled under the walls and lying along the roads were beyond count. The dead were left unburied and the air was polluted by the stench of rotting bodies. Hideous corruption was often too much for the eye to bear. The rivers and fields were so clotted with cadavers, that horses and wagons could not find their way. The wood cutters did not have the strength to bring their wood to the city, and people began to chop up their own furnishings and go about peddling the splinters for faggots. Still, whatever a man could sell did not suffice to keep him alive for a single day. And then—most horrible of all—among the faggots offered for sale could often be seen splinters with red paint or bits of silver or gold foil still sticking to them: the temples had been violated! The wooden figures of Buddha, and the sacred vessels, had been stolen to be chopped up for firewood. O to have been born into such a muddy and degenerate world!

Every disaster could be measured on a personal scale. The lover and his beloved could not bear to be parted, and yet they must die. Of the two, the nobler would be the first to die, for the survival of the other being paramount, the one who loved more deeply—either the man or the woman—would reserve for the beloved the few crumbs which begging availed. A certain high priest from one of the temples, deploring the fact that so many men died without last rites, rallied his fellow monks, and with them walked among the dead placing upon their foreheads the sacred A of Amida and consigning them to Buddha.

A like disaster is said to have occurred during the reign of the Emperor Sutoku[1]—but of those days and times I know very little; what I have seen has been quite enough.

In the second year of the era of Ganryaku,[2] the earth was racked by a tremendous quaking. This disaster was of no ordinary proportions. Entire mountains crumbled and slid into the rivers below. The sea rose up and spilled over the land. The earth gaped open and the waters churned with swirling froth. Cliffs were rent and crashed with the roar of thunder into the valleys. Boats were piled high and dry upon the

---

[1] 1124 - 1141 A.D.
[2] 1185 A.D.

land, and of the roads not enough remained for a horse to keep his footing.

In the capital, no house, no temple, no shrine, no tomb was spared; if they were not flattened, they crumbled. Ashes and dust spiraled up like billows of smoke, and the rumbling of the earth and the crashing of houses sounded like thunder. No man knew what to do: if he stayed inside he was crushed; outside, he was swallowed by the earth. A man has not the wings of a bird to fly with, nor can he ride up to the heavens on a cloud as the dragon does. One of the most pathetic cases was that of a child of six or seven, the only son of a certain samurai, who was caught in a tiny playhouse which he had built under the eaves of his father's house. He was buried under the collapsing house and his little body smashed. His eyes protruded nearly an inch from their sockets. How awful it was to see the grief-crazed parents carrying the body of their dead child and hear their anguished cries! Even the pride and dignity of a samurai must give way before such pain as this.

After the violence of the first shock had diminished, secondary tremors continued for a long while. Usually not a day passed without twenty or thirty strong tremblors. Gradually they came less frequently; at first, four or five times a day, then two or three, finally once every two or three days. At last they stopped altogether. Certain it is that of all the disasters which descend on this world—flood, fire, and tempest included—none can so change the face of the earth as a mighty temblor. It is said that long ago, in the era of Saiko, a tremendous earthquake shook the land so severely that in the Todai Temple the head of the great Buddha cracked off and tumbled to the floor.

And so it has ever been. In this world nothing is constant. We ourselves, and our dwellings too, are inconstant. What grief must a man endure to gain status or establish a home!

If a man of low station place himself under the protection of another, he may thereby obtain certain advantage, but he will never be assured enduring peace. If he should suffer some misfortune, he can not, in deference to his master, raise his voice or cry out in grief. He is always worried about promotion or disgrace, and even his movements must be guarded, lest they offend. Indeed, he is like a sparrow too close to the nest of the hawk.

And a poor man can not live in peace as neighbour to a rich man. Day and night he is aware of his shabbiness. He feels unable to come or go without offering the tribute of adulation. His heart is never at ease, because he is conscious of his neighbour's disdain and of the envy of his own wife and household.

If a man live in a narrow crowded street, how can he avoid sorrow or loss if a fire break out in his quarter. If he live in an out-of-the-way section, it is inconvenient to get about, and he must live in constant fear of robbers.

A man of ambition is immured in greed and ambition.

A man who lives alone is despised by his fellows.

A man of possessions is prey to endless trouble.

A man who has little is gnawed by constant anxiety.

If a man accept the protection of another, he becomes that man's slave.

If a man offer protection to another, he exposes himself to entangling sentiments.

If a man accept the ways of the world, he violates himself.

If a man rejects its ways, he is considered mad.

What can a man do? Where should he live? Where can he seek refuge? Where can he know peace even for the span of a jade-bell's tinkle?

## III

For many years I lived in the home of my father's mother. When she died, my health deteriorated, and I moved away. I was just past thirty. I had too long endured the malevolence of men. Following my own counsel, I built a small dwelling apart, no more than one-tenth the size of the residence I had just quitted. It was large enough only for the barest living, and had no extra rooms. I raised a kind of wall, but was not able to afford a gate. The framework was of bamboo, and when finished, my dwelling looked a bit like a wagon-shelter. When the wind blew and the snow fell, it was not undangerous. The river was close by and the threat of a flood was constant. Marauders roamed at will.

Here I meditated upon the emptiness of man's desires. How well I knew the briefness of man's span upon this earth! How many disasters had I not witnessed!

My decision was made; and as I greeted my fiftieth spring, I turned my back on the world forever.

I had no wife or child to make my renunciation difficult. I had no official duties to perform. I did not even have a salary to tempt me. There was nothing to hold me to the world. And so I left. And for several springs and autumns I lay idly amid the clouds on the slopes of Mount Ohara.

19

Here, my life now fleeting as the dew, I reached my sixtieth year. And here, once again, I raised my shelter, as impermanent as the autumn leaf. It was the sort of hut a hunter would build to protect himself for a single night. It was like the fragile cocoon of some aged silkworm. It was not even one-hundredth the size of my former dwelling.

As my life waxes in years, my dwellings wane in size. This house of mine was not at all like the usual habitation of this world. It measured barely ten-feet square, and the ceiling was not seven feet high. Since I had no particular desire to remain in one spot, I did not even secure the structure to the earth. I raised rude walls and covered the roof with thatch. The joints were fixed with wooden pegs. Thus, if I so fancied, I might easily move the whole structure to another spot and re-assemble it there. No more than two carts would be needed to transport the whole of it, and except for the wagon-fee, there would be no expense involved.

Thus exiled, of my own will, among the recesses of Mount Hino, I continued to work on my abode. To the south, I hung a bamboo sun screen over a small porch; to the west, I built a small altar and above it I reverently hung a scroll with Amida's image so that the rays of the setting sun shone squarely on his forehead. Beside the curtained door I placed the images of Fugen and Fudo.[1] Above the paper sliding-door to the north, I built a tiny shelf, and placed upon it three or four leather boxes in which I put my poems, my music, my book on the Western Paradise, and other writings.

On one side of my room I placed my Chinese lute and on the other my biwa. The lute folds to take less room and the biwa, which is joined with pegs, can be taken apart. On the east I laid out my bed of straw and fern. On the same side a small writing table stands before a window. Near my pillow is a brazier in which to burn faggots. North of my house is a small garden surrounded by a low hedge, and there I plant my medicinal herbs. This is my humble and impermanent abode.

Let me tell of my days here. To the south is a tiny stone-lined pool where the rain water collects. The forest is only as distant as the edge of my roof and firewood is but a step away. The mountain is called Toyama. The never-fading ivy grows so thickly that the traces of men are in-

---

[1] *Fugen* (普賢)
Buddhist Divinity, a patron of those who practice Hokke Zammai (Ecstatic Contemplation). His statue is often placed on the right of Sakyamuni's.

*Fudo* (不動)
Buddhist Divinity having the power to counteract the spells of demons. He is fierce of visage and usually represented as surrounded by flames. In his right hand he carries a blade for striking devils and in his left hand a rope to strangle them.

visible. Though the valleys are heavily wooded, the way is open to the west, where lies the Buddha's Paradise. How often in my meditations do my thoughts fly there.

In the spring, the hills to the west, covered by waves of wisteria, are like purplish clouds, and their scent delights my nostrils. In the summer I hear the incessant calling of the whipoorwills as they speak their promise to follow one another along Death's High Road.[1] In the autumn, my ears are filled with the cicada's chirping. I cannot tell if he only grieves for his cast away moult or if he laments too the pains of this mortal world. In winter my heart is filled with emotion as I watch a snowfall. I liken the falling and melting flakes to the sins of men. They form and fade away before the Buddha's compassion.

When I am weary of meditating or reading the sutras, I rest as I please. There is no one to hinder me in my whims, no friend to reproach me my laziness. I have no need for vows of silence. Solitude deters a wagging tongue. The commandments are safe with me here, for so far from men, what reasons have I to break them?

In the mornings as I watch the boats plying their way up the river, I am reminded by the white billows in their wakes of the evanescence of my own life, and I am moved by the elegance of Manshami's[1] beautiful verse. And in the evening, when the wind plays upon the leaves of the Judas tree, I seem to see the waters of Jinyo, the abode of gentle Li-Po, and I play my lute in the ancient manner of Gentoku. Sometimes with the melody called *Winds of Autumn* I accompany the rustling of the pine leaves; sometimes I seek to merge the music of the *Flowing Spring* with the sounds of the rushing water outside my door. I am very inexpert in all this, but then I play for no other man's ear. I play for myself. I sing for myself. My own heart is my only audience.

At the foot of my mountain stands a humble brushwood hut, the abode of the forest warden. His young son comes occasionally to visit me. Our time is our own, and we often take long walks together. We enjoy each other's company. He is sixteen and I am sixty. The difference in our

---

[1] *Death's High Road* (Shide No Yama 死出の山)
A hill, or a road passing over it, in the Buddhist Hades. Souls pass over it on the way to Paradise or Hell.

[1] *Manshami* ( 䵝 伜 䵝 )
A celebrated poet of the eighth century who entered a religious order in grief for the sickness of the Emperor. The reference is to the following poem:

| Yo No Naka Wo | To what shall I |
| Nani Ni Tatoemu | Compare this World? |
| Asaborake | — To the Whitening Wake |
| Kogiyuku Fune No | that Trails my Boat |
| Ato No Shiranami | in the Morning's Glow. |

ages is considerable, yet the pleasure we exchange in our hearts knows no age.

Sometimes we go out to pluck the succulent reeds, sometimes to pick mountain pears. We may gather up the rice bran or pluck wild parsley, or sometimes go down to the fields to search for the ears of corn which the farmers have overlooked. I make them into bundles to dry for my table. If the weather is fine we climb high upon the rocks and gaze off at the far distant sky over my native place. Dimly in the distance I see Kohatayama and the villages of Fushimi, Toha, and Hatsukashi. These scenes are mine as well as any man's, for no man can say he owns the view nor can he deprive me of the pleasure it gives me.

Walking is one of my pleasures. When my spirit yearns for distant places I set out from my mountain and follow the hazy line of the hill tops. I cross over Sumiyama and pass by Kasatori hill where I delay a few moments to pray at the shrine at Iwama. If I please, I seek the temple of Ishiyama to bow before the sacred image of Kwannon. Or again, I may cross the fields of Awazu to honor the grave of the sage Semimaru.[1] Perhaps I will cross Tagami river to pay respects at the tomb of Sarumaru,[2] the poet of old. When my steps turn homeward, I may, as the season permits, fill my eyes with the beauties of cherry blossoms or gather the fire-filled leaves of the maple, or cut sprigs from fragrant ferns, or pick the full-ripened fruit. My prizes I sometime offer to Buddha, sometimes carry home for my own pleasure.

In the quiet of night when the moon's rays steal through my window, I think of all the great men of old, and the sleeves of my robe are wet with tears. Through my window I see bands of fleeting sparks, and I think: are they fire flies in a nearby thicket or the fishing fires off distant Maki island? How like the murmur of the wind through the trees is the patter of the rain at dawn! The call of a pheasant reaches my ear. Its soft notes awake, now the memory of my mother, now that of my father. The wild deer who frolic at the foot of my mountain remind me of how distant I am from the civilization of man. Stirring up the embers of the fire, I half awaken from my old man's slumber. An owl calls and its

---

[1] *Semimaru* (蟬丸)

A blind retainer of Prince Atsuzane-Shinno (897-966) son of the Emperor Uda, he was renowned for his poetry and music (biwa). He retired in his old age to Osaka (Yamashiro) and lived out his days in solitude. The younger son of the Emperor Daigo, desiring to be received as a pupil of the famed blind music master, prostrated himself every evening during three years before the door of the master's house without Semimaru's deigning to accept him as a pupil. Convinced at last by this extreme of perseverance, however, the master consented and the Prince was received.

[2] *Sarumaru* (猿丸)

Celebrated poet of the ninth century.

sadness fills my heart. All the beauties of nature are here on this mountain. And yet will all of them suffice to show a man the depths of his own heart?

IV

When I first came here to live, I thought of this only as a temporary abode, but already five years have passed. My improvised cabin has become an old house. Rotting leaves are piled high upon the eaves, and moss covers the ground on which it stands. Occasionally news reaches me from the city, and I learn that many men of high respect and station have died since my retirement to the mountain. I reflect on the countless thousands of men of low station who have also disappeared from the scene. How many houses I knew are now gone, devoured in the flames? And yet, my tiny and impermanent abode has provided me shelter all the while. I have lived in tranquility and untroubled by fear.

Most men would say that my abode is too cramped for living, but I find the floor ample enough for my slumber at night and it accommodates me adequately during the day. It affords ample space for a man alone. The hermit crab asks no more than its tiny shell. This is because it knows itself and understands its needs. Why does the osprey live on a storm swept crag? Because it fears men. So it is with me. I know myself and I know the world. I ask nothing from it. I would have no intercourse with it. My only prayer is for tranquillity. My pleasure is in freedom from care.

It is traditional that every man build for himself a dwelling in this world. But how often is what he has built really for himself? A man often builds for his family or his kin, or for his friends or his relatives, or for his lord or his masters, or even for his treasures or his livestock. He builds for any or all of these but seldom for himself. But I, this time, have built for myself alone and for no other man. My reason is simple enough. I have found no one, peer or servant, whom I would care to have with me. Why therefore should I build for anyone but myself?

Among men it is the wealthy who are respected and those of fine manners who are most honoured. The man of heart is seldom accepted. As for me, I take for my closest friends my music, the flowers, and the moon. Of servants I have no need, for their thoughts are only for themselves and they give their respect only to those who bestow favour. Kindness and good treatment alone are never sufficient. I myself am my only servant.

23

If there is something that need be done, I do it myself, for 'though the task may be fatiguing, yet it is less so than watching another do the work for me. If it is necessary to walk a long distance, then I walk myself, for though it may be troublesome, yet it will grieve me less than the labour of the horse who carries me or the oxen who pulls my cart.

I have assigned my body a double function. My hands I have made my servant and my legs my conveyance. They are both in close attunement with my heart. My heart, knowing all too well the grievances of my body, gives it rest when it is afflicted and orders it to work when it is strong. Though the body be sometimes dull or out of sorts, the heart is never perturbed for the two are in perfect harmony. It goes without saying that much walking and movement is nourishing to the mind as well as body. Why should a man waste time in idleness? When we grieve or trouble another being, we do eternal injury to ourselves. How then can we with tranquil heart make use of another man's labor?

I do not seek for the favour of others even for food and clothing. My robe I wove myself from wisteria bark, my night covers are of woven hemp. I cover my body with whatever I can contrive. Wild reeds from the field and nuts from the mountain trees give me all I need. I have no dealings with other men, so why should I be ashamed of my appearance? And the very scarcity of my humble and crude fare lends it sweetness. I have not written all this to persuade others to my ways. I speak only for myself as I compare my lot with what I knew before.

Since I turned my back on this world and abandoned all its false ways, I have felt no regret, nor known any fear. I have placed myself in Fortune's keeping. Without regret, without spite, I am as free as the drifting cloud. My earthly pleasures are those provided me by the changing beauties of nature. My greatest joy comes in that tranquil moment when, head on pillow, I pass away to my slumber.

In this world the heart is all. If one's heart is unquiet, not castles nor horses, nor all the seven treasures of Buddha will avail to make a man glad; and palaces and mansions will have no meaning for him. In this lonely dwelling, my hut of a single room, I have found peace. I must naturally go forth into the city from time to time, and when I do, I feel some shame because of my beggarly appearance. Yet when I return here to my hut, I feel only pity for those men whose lives are mired in the morass of this world.

If my words ring false for any man, I can only bid him remark the ways of the birds and fishes. The fish never tires of the water; and yet, not being a fish, how can one tell how a fish feels in its heart? The bird

24

ever seeks the tree; and yet, not being a bird how can one tell how a bird feels in its heart? So it is with the secluded life. Who can perceive its charms who has not lived alone?

And so my life wanes like the moon approaching the rim of the hill which will hide it. Soon I must face the three domains of darkness. And there how shall I regard my life? The purport of Buddha's words is this: Let not your heart cling to the things of this world. Thus, it is a sin to love even this hut of straw. Even my pleasure in this life of peace is a hindrance to my salvation. Why, then, should I pass these last days extolling this empty pleasure?

In the quiet of the early morning's light I meditated upon this theme, and to my heart I posed this question:

You have turned from the world and come here to live amid the forests of this mountain in order to bring peace to your heart and walk in the way of Buddha. But though you appear a holy man, yet your heart is confused. Though this dwelling of yours is copied after the hut of Jomyo Koji,[1] yet in virtue you have barely the merit of Shuri Handoku.[2] Have you fallen so low because your heart is afflicted by the poverty and mean station which your Karma has allotted you, or has the blindness of your heart driven you mad?

My heart had no answer to give. I could only move my tongue wearily to repeat thrice the holy name of Buddha. No more.

*Written in his hut on Toyama by the Somon Ren-In on the last day of the third month in the year two of the era called Ganryaku.*

The waning moon soon sinks behind
the mountain's rim.
Would that I might regard her radiant
face forever.

終

*Kamo Chomei*

(Translated by Thomas Rowe and Anthony Kerrigan)

_____

[1] *Jomyo Koji* (淨名居士)

Vimalakirtti, a contemporary of Sakyamuni. He lived in a hut just ten feet square. The model for Chomei's dwelling. He is said to have performed the miracle of making room for all 3000 saints and 500 disciples of Buddha assembled within his tiny cabin.

[2] *Shuri Handoku* (周利槃特)

The most foolish of all Buddha's disciples. He could memorize none of the sutras for as he memorized one line he would forget the preceding. He is said to have been unable to remember his own name. A kind of ginger grew on his grave which destroyed the memory of those who ate it.

Kinesics is the study of the visually sensible aspects of non-verbal, inter-personal communication. It is divided into three units: *Pre-kinesics* deals with general physiological, pre-communicational aspects of body motion. *Micro-kinesics* is concerned with the derivation of kines (least particles of isolatable body-motion) into manageable morphological classes. And *social kinesics* is concerned with these morphological constructs as they relate to communication.

## Pre-kinesics

Present research in kinesics is proceeding upon, and limited by, the assumption that visually perceptible body shifts, whose variations have been repetitively observed and are subject to systematization, are learned. This assumption does not preclude consideration of physiological influence. Generalizations about individual variations of velocity and intensity must await more definitive neuro-muscular and endocrine research. But failure to keep pre-kinesics separate from micro-kinesics and social kinesics leads to reductionism. In the early stages of investigation, important data were overlooked by being dumped into the wastepaper baskets of 'an itch', 'weariness', 'muscular relaxation', 'tonus', and the like. But such stimuli to body movement are often, if not usually, de-

26

pendent upon the context of the act and its social definition. To 'scratch', to 'shift', to 'stretch', to 'relax', and to 'tense' are but a few of many apparently simple physiological reactions which are socially defined and controlled. To equivocate by calling them psychosomatic is to sacrifice experimental clarity for interdisciplinary fellowship.

In this discussion I shall use the closing and opening of the lids of one eye for illustration. This example contains much behaviour which is non-significant (at the present) to kinesiological research. For instance, a high speed camera records almost a thousand positions of the lid in closing and opening, A graph derived from such a film strip shows rests, reverses, and velocity shifts which are imperceptible to the unassisted eye. Any society 'selects' but a portion of this range for interactional definition. The remainder may be described as 'artifacts of selection', if they can be shown to have, in a given population, no more than *discriminational meaning*, which is present when an observer reports the ability to distinguish B from A and/or C in a series.

The least isolated particle we call a *kine*. Members of a group use only certain of the discriminated range of kines for social interaction. While the range of discrimination certainly relates to experience, and while we have varying ranges of kines for differing groups, only certain kines seem to have traceable *differential meaning*. Differential meaning occurs when informants repetitively report that the variation in placement, intensity, or position of a kine 'changes the meaning' of a set or continuum.

*Micro-kinesics*

Micro-kinesics deals with the systematization of kines with differential meaning into manageable morphological classes. It will be evident from the example that, while morphology initially complicates the research, ultimately it reduces the body of data. To jump from discriminational meaning to social meaning leaves us encumbered with a load of non-significant kines. Micro-kinesics research ensures the establishment of differentially significant units which may then be tested for contextual meanings. In a series of tests, five young nurses reported they could discriminate eleven positions of lid closure (eleven kines with discriminational meaning). All agreed that only four 'meant' anything (four kines with differential meaning). Retesting of the nurses revealed that the latter were not precise positions, but ranges of positions, which the nurses reported as 'open-eyed', 'droopy-lidded', 'squinting', and 'eyes squeezed tight', all of which they distinguished from 'just open' and 'closed'. We define the positions within the range as *allokinic*; each class of allokines, or variants within a range, we define as a *kineme*.

27

During the test the actor does his best not to vary other musculature than are immediately involved in the kine series. This is difficult but can often be done. Once the kines, allokines, and kinemes are established, the researcher is equipped to begin morphological analysis. By acting out or pointing out a combination of kines in various pre-established areas, he checks for functional relationships between kinemes. For example, in working with the nurses we established the presence of thirty-four kines relating to the position of the eyebrows. The nurses reported that twenty-three of these had differential meaning. In a culture which emphasizes 'looking one in the eyes' and 'taking things at face value', this multiplicity is not surprising. Preliminary work with German, Japanese, and Bombay Hindu informants indicates a much narrower range in this body area.

Consequent to this research, it was found that only one of the five nurses could reproduce more than five of the twenty-three positions which they recognized to have differential meaning. Using a male control group of college students of comparable age, it was established that all could reproduce at least ten, with an average of fifteen. One extremely versatile young man produced thirty-five kines and easily got the twenty-three with differential meaning. Significantly, far less sex difference was noted in the ability of our Japanese and German informants. (This may be related to the small number of informants in the non-American groupings.) From this experiment, alone, we feel we have isolated significant recognition and reproduction differences within the informant range and between sexes. Just as we have a larger reading and hearing vocabulary than we do a speaking one, so we may have a larger viewing than acting list. Parenthetically, only morphological research has given us any feeling of security in describing any particular motion as *idiokinesic*.

To return to our methodological procedure. As soon as it was discovered that the variation of one or the other of the kines in a given area in the composite changed the differential meaning of the composite, we described the abstracted combination as a kinemorph. For example, 'droopy-lidded' combined with 'bilaterally raised, median portion depressed brows' has an evident differential meaning from the former combined with a 'low unilateral brow lift'. It was noted that variation from left to right was non-kinemic so long as companion brows and eyes were involved. Thus, right and left composite positions are *allokinomorphs* which may be generalized into a single *kinomorpheme*.

When kinemorphs from all parts of the body and/or in series (i.e., through time) are seen to be functionally related, the whole is described

28

as a *kinemorphic construction*. At each step we are further liberated from the unnecessary tedium of kine recording when doing later communication research.

The discovery that the variation of *either* brow or lids may vary the differential meaning of the kinemorph, relieves us from the over-easy temptation, at least at this stage, of indulging in discussion concerning modifiers and subjects or predicators. Nevertheless, I have a hunch that cross-cultural research is going to lead to the development of kinesic syntax. Present research seems to indicate that in middle-majority American culture circum-eye movement takes priority in definition of situation over movement of the hands, the arms, the trunk, and even over the head. This becomes apparent when we compare such data with that derived from Southern European and Southeast Asian informants.

Let me illustrate several of these points with an excerpt from an experiment:

Left eye closed; right open
Left orbital margin squinted
Mouth held in 'normal'
Tip of nose depressed (bunnynose)

(This projection held for no more than five seconds. Retest with shorter duration.)

Right eye closed; left open
Left orbital margin squinted
Mouth held in 'normal'
Tip of nose depressed (bunnynose)

Informant's remark: 'They look different but they wouldn't mean anything different.'
Tentative analysis: Shift from closing of right eye to left eye does not shift meaning. Leftness and rightness allokinic in this case. Use of unilateral squint unnoticed by informant.

Left eye closed; right open
Mouth held in 'normal'
Tip of nose depressed
Neither orbital margin squinted
Informant's remark: 'That's the same as the first.'
Tentative analysis: Squint morphologically insignificant.

Left eye closed; right open
Left orbital margin squinted (or unsquinted)
Mouth drawn into pout
Tip of nose depressed
Informant's remark: 'Well, that changes things.'
Tentative analysis: Mouth position morphologically significant.

Here are two examples of recording situations. Both were taken in context, one on a bus, the second in a home. In only the second was there any direct information other than that supplied by the situation itself. Except insofar as there are regional cultural differences in the United States, these can be described as members of the common American culture. Mother and child spoke with a Tidewater, Virginia accent. The hostess is a native of Cleveland, Ohio, resident in Washington since 1945; the guest is from a small Wisconsin town and is presently residing in Chicago. Both the hostess and the guest could probably be assigned an upper middle class position as measured by a Warner-type analysis. The bus route on which the bus event was recorded leads to a similar neighbourhood. The way in which the mother and child were dressed was not consistent with the other riders who disembarked, as did the observer, before the mother and child did. Both the hostess and her guest were in their late thirties. The child was about four, while his mother seemed to be about twenty-seven to thirty.

In Figures 1 and 2 stress and intonation are indicated above the pertinent text, using symbols provided in Trager and Smith's *Outline of English Structure;* voice-qualifiers, e.g., the drawl ( ⌒ ) are indicated by symbols developed by them. In a few places a phonemic transcription of the text is also provided. Kinesic symbols are given below the pertinent text, but merely illustrated, not translated. Those interested in a more detailed analysis are referred to the author's *Introduction to Kinesics*, University of Louisville Press.

1. This situation was observed on a street at about 2:30 p.m., April 14. The little boy was seated next to the window. He seemed tired of looking out of the window and, after surveying all of the car ads and the passengers, he leaned toward his mother and pulled at her sleeve, pouted and vigorously kicked his legs.

2. His mother had been sitting erectly in her seat, her packages on her lap, and her hands lightly clasped around the packages. She was apparently 'lost in thought'.

3. When the boy's initial appeal failed to gain the mother's attention, he began to jerk at her sleeve again, each jerk apparently stressing his vocalization.

4. The mother turned and looked at him, 'shushed' him, and placed her right hand firmly across his thighs.

5. The boy protested audibly, clenched both fists, pulled them with stress against his chest. At the same time he drew his legs up against the restraint of his mother's hand. His mouth was drawn down and his upper face was pulled into a tight frown.

6. The mother withdrew her hand from his lap and resettled in her former position with her hands clasped around the packages.

7. The boy grasped her upper arm tightly, continued to frown. When no immediate response was forthcoming, he turned and thrust both knees into the lateral aspect of her left thigh.

8. She looked at him, leaned toward him, and slapped him across the anterior portion of his upper legs.

9. He began to jerk his clenched fists up and down, vigorously nodding between each inferior-superior movement of his fists.

10. She turned, frowning, and with her mouth pursed, she spoke to him through her teeth. Suddenly she looked around, noted that the other passengers were watching, and forced a square smile. At the same time that she finished speaking, she reached her right hand in under her left arm and squeezed the boy's arm. He sat quietly.

1. Child: Mama. I gotta go to the bathroom.
   (mo) o o   L35⌐  m8ther's sleeve   2
                                       x

2. Mother:
   T '• •⁺ 1 8 X X 1  ʎmʎ 3-3-3

3. Child: Mama. Donnie's gotta go.
   R35⌐   R35⌐   R35⌐R35⌐R35⌐
   mo. r. sleeve

4. Mother:  Sh-sh.
   R5 across child's lap - firm through 5

5. Child: But  mama.
   XX41

6. Mother:  Later.   (o openness; ⱴ over-softness)
   1 8 X X 1  o o

7. Child:  mah  mah   (⋀ over-loudness ≈ whine)
   R5   ʎʎ zz  against mother's thigh
   mother's arm

8. Mother: Wait.   (ʔ rasp)
   R14⌐ against child's thighs

9. Child: Oh  mama,  mama,  mama.   4máh4/1máh#
   XX41 ↑ __H__ ↓ ↑   ↓   ↑   H

10. Mother: Shut  up.  Will  yuh.
    h        L35  child's l. u. arm
                  behind own r. arm

32

Guest of honour forty-five minutes late. Three couples waiting, plus host and hostess. Host had arranged guest list for function.

1. As the hostess opened the door to admit her guest, she smiled a closed-toothed smile. As she began speaking she drew her hands, drawn into loose fists, up between her breasts. Opening her eyes very wide, she then closed them slowly and held them closed for several words. As she began to speak she dropped her head to one side and then moved it toward the guest in a slow sweep. She then pursed her lips momentarily before continuing to speak, indicating that he should enter.

2. He looked at her fixedly, shook his head, and spread his arms with his hands held open. He then began to shuffle his feet and raised one hand, turning it slightly outward. He nodded, raised his other hand, and turned it palm-side up as he continued his vocalization. Then he dropped both hands and held them, palms forward, to the side and away from his thighs. He continued his shuffling.

3. She smiled at him, lips pulled back from clenched teeth. Then, as she indicated where he should put his coat, she dropped her face momentarily into an expressionless pose. She smiled toothily again, clucked and slowly shut, opened, and shut her eyes again as she pointed to the guest with her lips. She then swept her head from one side to the other. As she said the word 'all' she moved her head in a sweep up and down from one side to the other, shut her eyes slowly again, pursed her lips, and grasped the guest's lapel.

4. The guest hunched his shoulders, which pulled his lapel out of the hostess' grasp. He held his coat with both hands, frowned, and then blinked rapidly as he slipped the coat off. He continued to hold tightly to his coat.

1. Hostess: Oh we were afraid you werent coming but# good#
R1121   #5)(5-R1

2. Guest: Im very sorry# got held up# you know calls
shuffle
2  and all that#
-shuffle 5)(5

3. Hostess: Put your wraps here# People are dying to
R113
#
meet you# Ive told them all about you.
R113 through 'have'
guest's lapel

4. Guest: You have well I dont know# Yes# No# I'd love
removes coat   clutches coat
2  to meet them#

*Social Kinesics*

Social kinesics deals with body motion units with contextual meaning, the context being provided by the social situation. Now in this discussion I have avoided the word 'gesture' for gesture is restricted to those acts or actions whose descriptions contain vocalized rationalizations by the actor or viewer. Research has revealed, however, that gestures are no more 'meaningful' than other acts. The subjective, vocalized meanings attached to them do not necessarily supply us with insight into either the differential or the contextual meaning of the kinemorphic construction or action, of which the gesture is an independent but deceptively visible aspect. Consider the variety of messages relayed by an action of which the 'thumbed-nose' is the *explicit* focus. The delusory availability of gestures has provided the same handicap to the development of kinesics that formal grammar has to the understanding of linguistics. The most successful research in the field of kinesics has come from the attempt to understand the relationship between visible and audible communication. New developments in linguistics, pioneered by Smith and Trager, make possible the organic relationship between such phonema; particularly intonation patterns, phrase superfixes, and voice qualifiers. So intimate is this relationship that the trained linguist-kinsiologist has at times been able to describe many of the movements of a speaker from hearing a recording or listening to a telephone conversation. Further, we have found that an auditor may 'hear' intonational shifts which were not spoken but *moved* by the informant, and vice versa. Yet these phenomena are not inseparable. Smith and Trager have described as *meta-incongruent* the situation which occurs when the subjective meaning carried by the words in an utterance are contradicted by the intonation or voice-qualifiers used with it. A comparable situation occurs when the utterance has one contextual meaning and the accompanying action another. The utilization of such data has evident value for interviewers. Meta-incongruences are as important for those interested in 'unconscious behaviour' as in the recognition that there occur kinesic 'slips' and 'stuttering'.

Of more interest perhaps to the non-linguist is the working process of in-group conversation. As part of a study of an adolescent clique, we paid particular attention to the 'origin-response ratio'. Three of the nine boys in this group were, by word count, heavy vocalizers. In fifteen recorded scenes (five scenes for each of the three), they were responsible for from seventy-two to ninety-three percent *of the words* spoken. One of the three was regarded by the group as a leader. (Incidentally, he originated more conversations or new trends to conversation than any

35

of the other boys.) But the other recognized leader had one of the lowest word count percentages of the group. He originated, by our count, at a median rate, but he spoke only about sixteen percent of the words. His leadership seemed to be a kinesic one.

Compared with the other boys, he engaged in few unrelated acts, that is, acts not traceably related to the interactional chain. (These 'unrelated acts' appear to be abortive efforts to originate action; they seem related to similar behaviour in smaller children except that older children more frequently realize when the group is not responsive.) Compared with the adults in the neighbourhood, he was kinesically more 'mature' than the other boys. He engaged in less 'foot shuffling', 'dramatic thought'—a substitution (?) of kinemorphic constructions for verbal descriptions was characteristic of this group,—and he exhibited fewer hand-mouth kinemorphic constructions than his peers. Even though he vocalized relatively little, he was known as a good conversationalist. Kinesiological analysis of this boy revealed that he was a 'good listener'. His reponses were seldom meta-incongruent, he steered the conversation with face and head kinemorphs, and he seldom engaged in leg and foot 'jiggling' which generally conveys a contextual meaning of restlessness, malaise, or negation.

*Ray L. Birdwhistell*

## UTOPIA AND COUNTER-UTOPIA

The dream of a society drastically altered has haunted Western thought from the time of Plato. This dream has two main forms: one is a wish-fulfilment and the other a nightmare. In both versions human life is much more thoroughly ordered and controlled than it is in actuality. Where this control appears benevolent, we have the vision of utopia. Where it appears malevolent, we have what I would call counter-utopia. A fantasy of counter-utopia is expressed in the following story by a little girl of eight:

Once upon a time there was a very solemn town in which the children could not play. I mean they could play, but they could not play together, the girls with the boys and the boys with the girls. The children did not like that but it was the rule and they had to follow it. Every girl wore a pink or white or yellow or green dress, and could never, never, never, never even think of playing with boys. The boys wore black or brown or blue polo shirts and pants. The girls could only play hopscotch, jump rope and other girlish games like that. The boys could only play football and baseball and games like that. The houses were solemn too. Every house had a high chimney and a path, a door square like any door, and the windows were round. The smoke came out of the chimneys in

37

circles like chains. If it didn't come out like that the people were killed. Awful rules, aren't they? But usually it came out in ringlets. Everyone had one acre of ground with pine trees, and they had to have roses. The town was funny though the people who lived there didn't think so. One day the girls went blackberry picking and they met the boys who were going out hunting bears and deer. Soon, before they knew it, the boys were playing with the girls and the girls were playing with the boys. They both played Ring-o-leavio. In our school both boys and girls play it, but in that place it was only a boys' game. And they came home and their mothers said, 'Where have you been? Have you been playing with boys?' And the boys' fathers said, 'Have you been playing with girls?' The boys had stains of pink and white from the clothes of the girls. In that country the clothes were sticky. And the girls' clothes had brown and black on them. And they were all spanked and sent to bed, feeling very bad, without any supper.

This child's story of a solemn town contains most of the major features of utopias and counter-utopias. Life is strictly regulated down to minute details by authorities who can detect any violation. Control is applied particularly to the relations between the sexes. Similar control is provided for in the classical utopias and is a focus for rebellion in the counter-utopias. In Plato's Republic, mating was to be strictly supervised by the guardians of the state. It was to occur only at special hymeneal celebrations. Only those of certain ages were eligible. In order to breed the best stock, strong and brave warriors were given the most access to the women. Men of less desirable qualities were denied the opportunity. The guardians were to maintain the deception that sexual privileges were determined by lot, while they would manipulate the lots in the interests of improving the breed. All children were to be separated from their mothers from birth, and no one was to know his own children or his own parents. In More's Utopia, anyone who had premarital intercourse was denied the right ever to marry. Adultery was punished by consignment to life-long slavery.

To Plato and to More such stringent regulation of sexual life appeared a desirable and benevolent arrangement. To have wayward sexual impulses subjected to the control of severe but good authorities seemed to them a necessary condition of a reasonable and virtuous existence. Such a longing for benevolent restraint is not entirely alien to our contemporaries. I was talking the other day with a young man about psychoanalysis. We had heard that in an earlier phase of psychoanalytic practice the analyst sometimes forebade the patient to have sexual relations during the course of the analysis. I remarked that this must have roused intense resistance in the patient. But my young friend said rather wistfully that he sometimes wished his analyst would tell him not to sleep with any more girls.

Utopian thinkers in their preoccupation with control express a fear of impulses. What is the image they have of the condition to which unleashed impulse would carry men? More describes a savage tribe who are neighbours to the Utopians. They care for nothing but fighting and killing. They have little loyalty to their allies since in their bloodthirsty frenzy they may turn against those on their own side. They sell their services as mercenaries though few survive to collect their fee. Plato draws a picture of the tyrannical man, whose character is the counterpart of the worst governed state. Dominated by irrational impulses, he turns against his own parents for the sake of a dancing girl or a handsome youth. He crowns his career of vice by beating his old father. Thus what is feared if sex is not subjected to rigid control is that the associated aggressive impulses will break through. And as Plato makes explicit, the aggression may turn against paternal authority. In utopian societies, paternal authorities are idealized; the restraints which they impose are accepted out of love and awe of them, and out of fear of one's own impulses. Ernst Kris has remarked that in utopias there is a high degree of inhibition of aggression which produces a sense of limitation, tameness, and colourlessness of personality. This colourlessness has its counterpart in the clothes of More's Utopians, which are uniformly of the same drab coarse cloth. Bellamy's Boston of the year 2000, in his *Looking Backward*, is pervaded by an unrelieved Sunday school atmosphere.

The counter-utopians see restrictive authority as cruel and frightening. For them the danger proceeds not from their own impulses but rather from the authorities who threaten terrible punishments for the pursuit of gratification. The careful ordering of life which for the utopians had such a noble and reassuring quality assumes a persecutory aspect. The regulation of sex provokes rebellion. Paternal authority, insidiously knowing all, attractive, malign, and indestructible, emerges as an agent of mutilation.

Eugene Zamiatin wrote *We* in 1923 in Russia, where it was not published. Zamiatin pictures the United State of one thousand years hence. People have no names but only numbers; all are dressed alike. The houses have glass walls, and a 'number' is permitted to lower the curtains of his room only for the 'sexual hour' with a partner for whom he has registered and on presentation of the appropriate pink slip to the house authority. A controlled promiscuity, in which each 'number' is eligible to have sexual hours with any 'number' of the opposite sex for whom he has registered, prevents intense attachments. Children are produced in some unspecified artificial way. The young are taught by robot instructors. All the 'numbers' work in unison, chew their synthetic food in the same rhythm, and march in ordered rows through the streets during the 'personal hour', the daily intermission from work.

The ruler of the United State is the Well-Doer, a man who seems to be made of iron, who is reelected every year in the ceremony of unanimity. The main public function of the Well-Doer is to execute an occasional deviant, such as a poet who gets the mad idea of writing poems of individual inspiration. Such a condemned criminal approaches voluntarily the instrument of execution, the Machine of the Well-Doer. The Well-Doer turns the switch, and the victim is in a moment reduced to a small puddle.

The scientists of the United State perfect an operation which will eliminate imagination; any wayward thought or dream which might disrupt the ordered efficiency of life will become impossible. The hero of the story, a highly placed engineer, becomes diverted from his initial complete acceptance of the regime when he falls in love with an impetuous, rebellious woman. The hero does not want to share this woman with other men, and becomes obsessed with dreams of her, a very disturbing phenomenon since he has never dreamed before. Through this woman he becomes involved in a revolutionary plot, which is eventually foiled. Brought before the Well-Doer, the hero, overawed, is told that he was only being used by the revolutionaries. He undergoes the operation for the removal of imagination, which has now become compulsory. As a result he can watch without a twinge of feeling while his former beloved is tortured to make her confess prior to her execution.

In Zamiatin's vision of a controlled society, paternal authority forbids intense love relations, which might lead to rebellion against him. To insure the submission of his subjects he inflicts on them a mutilating operation. A prized part of themselves must be removed to make them safely compliant. Similar ideas appear in Huxley's counter-utopias. In *Brave New World*, women are operated on to provide ovaries for the laboratory production of babies. Scientists tamper with the embryos to produce large batches of identical moronic twins to staff factories where they work in unison. Where everyone is produced out of a bottle, the

40

counterpart of mammy songs invokes nostalgically 'that dear little Bottle of mine'. Intensity of relations between men and women is avoided by compulsory promiscuity. To inculcate this idea there are 'solidarity services' where to the tune of 'Orgy-porgy' everyone makes love to whoever happens to be next to him in the circle. Here, as in Zamiatin's story, it is intense and exclusive love which motivates rebellion against the established order. An outsider, a 'savage', who was raised on an Indian reservation, has a mother to whom he is strongly attached, and falls in love with a girl in an old-fashioned idealizing, romantic way. Stimulated by his protest against the society, a poet and a scientist also become rebels and are exiled to remote islands, while the despairing savage commits suicide.

Huxley's *Ape and Essence* presents a grimmer prospect, in which sexual taboos and threats of mutilation are more explicit. The survivors of the future atomic wars live in dreary slavery except for the yearly sexual orgy. At all other times the women wear patches labeled 'No' over breasts, pubic region, and buttocks. Those of either sex who are impelled towards sexual activity out of season are called 'hots' and all evils in the state are blamed on them. The hero, a scientist from outside the state, falls in love with a girl whom he converts from seasonal, promiscuous sex to constant love. The head priest wants the scientist to join the sacred order, which, however, would require an operation, not entirely painless, castration. Under the pressure of the head priest's demands and the danger of being persecuted as a 'hot' the hero escapes with his girl beyond the borders of the state.

The relation to persecuting paternal authority is most fully elaborated in Orwell's *Nineteen Eighty-four*. From every wall of this England of the future the enlarged image of the ruler looks down; as the inscription states: 'Big Brother is watching you.' Every room is equipped with a two-way telescreen through which every move of the citizen can be observed by the authorities. Sex has been made joyless as no marriage between partners who betray any mutual attraction is approved. Rightminded young people belong to the Junior Anti-Sex League. Again, as in the previous stories, it is sexual love which motivates rebellion. The hero falls in love with a girl who, while outwardly conforming and wearing the badge of the Junior Anti-Sex League, enjoys sex and has developed great resourcefulness for the carrying on of a secret intrigue. The hero suffers from the drab routine of his life. He is unable to participate in the compulsory orgies of hate against the national enemy of the moment; rather he hates Big Brother. There is a high official towards whom he feels strongly attracted, who looks so intelligent, under-standing, possibly dissident. The hero finally meets this official who re-cruits him for a secret revolutionary group. It is of course all a ruse and, when the hero is arrested with his girl friend at one of their secret rendezvous, the official appears as his main inquisitor. The hero is laid out on a machine of which the official controls the switches, and is interrogated at length and subjected to intolerable pain whenever he gives the wrong answer. Nevertheless his positive feelings for the official persist; the official is so intelligent, so truly understanding. The aim of the interrogation is to make the hero betray his love for the girl and to become in his inmost feelings at one with the regime. When he is threatened with the one torture he could not bear, to have his face eaten up by starved rats, he cries out that they should do it to his beloved instead. Thus he is effectively disillusioned with his capacity to love a woman. When his instruction has advanced sufficiently, he is let out of prison for a while before he will be in the end physically liquidated. He spends most of his time sitting in a cafe drinking synthetic gin and working chess problems. He listens with increasing feeling to the broadcasts of war news. As the latest victory is announced, his eyes fill with tears. He looks up at the ever-present enormous face and finally feels that he loves Big Brother.

The good and bad dreams of a possible society, of utopia or counter-utopia, revolve around the ambiguous image of paternal authority. The father represents the demand that the little boy give up his first great love of a woman, his mother. This renunciation is achieved out of love of the father and fear of castration. Complying to an extreme degree with this paternal demand, Plato provided that in his ideal state no child would even know who his mother was. Parodying this demand, Huxley conjured up the Hatchery and Conditioning Centre in which babies are produced out of bottles. In utopian fantasies, the image of a compelling paternal figure who draws love to himself is positive. In the *Republic*, Socrates exercises a persuasive domination over the youths with whom he discourses, convincing them of the correctness of Plato's ideal state and himself embodying the type of philosopher-ruler to whom they would gladly submit. In Bellamy's *Looking Backward*, the hero submits to a hypnotist who puts him into such a deep sleep that he does not awaken for over a hundred years. He is thus prevented from marrying his fiancée. However, the result is beneficial as the hero can then live in the ideal state of the future, where he is mainly subjected to another spell-binding (or sleep-inducing) man, an elderly doctor who lectures him endlessly about the good society. In the counter-utopias, on the other hand, the forbidding and castrative aspect of paternal authority is in the ascendant. His very power of binding love to himself appears sinister. Zamiatin's Well-Doer with his Machine of liquidation and his compulsory operations, Huxley's World-Controllers interfering with romantic love, enforcing operations which prevent maternity, his high priests threatening castration, Orwell's beloved torturer rooting out the love of woman and enforcing the love of Big Brother all represent the father figure in his nightmare aspect.

Still another counter-utopia has recently appeared: Bernard Wolfe's *Limbo*. There, in an effort to control aggressive impulses, the young men become 'vol-amps', voluntary amputees, and the highest honour is given to those who have had all four limbs removed. Thus there seems to be a trend through time for counter-utopian writers to picture the threat of mutilation in increasingly drastic forms.

There are many issues of utopian speculation, notably the economic ones, which I have not discussed here. I have only considered the issue of impulses versus authority, and the alternative fantasies which arise depending on whether the one or the other is seen as the main danger. In our time the capacity for dreaming of ideal societies appears to have dwindled. This seems in part related to the emergence of totalitarian regimes in which control of individual life has been achieved to an unprecedented and frightening extent. Some of Zamiatin's fantasies, which might have seemed far-fetched in the years immediately following the Russian Revolution, have turned out to be prophetic. As the negative possibilities of controlled society materialized, it became more difficult to dream of its positive version. The nightmare of counter-utopia predominates.

*Martha Wolfenstein*

## NOTES ON THE CONCEPTION OF THE SELF AMONG THE WINTU INDIANS

The Wintu Indians of Northern California have a conception of the self which is markedly different from our own. I have attempted to arrive at this conception through an intensive analysis of linguistic form and structure, as well as a consideration of biographical texts and recorded mythical material. My study is incomplete, since I have no other record of actual behaviour. The ethnography of the Wintu as we have it, is an account of a dead and remembered culture. As a background to the Wintu material, I present occassionally linguistic clues to our own conception of the self.[1]

The definition of the self in our own culture rests on our law of contradiction. The self cannot be both self and not self, both self and other; the self excludes the other. Wintu philosophy in general has no law of contradiction. Where we have mutually exclusive dualistic categories, the Wintu have categories which are inclusive, but not mutually so; that is, object A will be included in object B, but not vice versa. Out of this context, B can be distinguished or emphasized through various linguistic devices. For example, in Wintu thought, man is included in nature; natural law, time-

[1] This is a revision of an article which appeared in *The Journal of Abnormal and Social Psychology*, 45:3, 1950.

less order, is basic and true, irrespective of man.[1] However, independent judgment, private experience and free will are not thereby excluded, but function transiently within the framework of natural law; man actualizes and gives temporality and concreteness to the natural order upon which he impinges—through act of will and personal intent.[2] Again, the generic is primary to the particular and includes it; the individual is particularized transiently, but is not set in opposition.[3] Again what may seem at first encounter to be suffixes of mutual exclusiveness, appear upon investigation to be different kinds of emphatics.[4] Even the equivalents of *either* and *or* are emphatics, pre-supposing inclusiveness or increase. The concept of the self forms one of these non-exclusive categories. When speaking about Wintu culture, we cannot speak of the self *and* society, but rather of the self *in* society. As a member of my society, writing for readers of this cultural background, I am presenting my study from the point of view of the self and its gradually decreasing participation in the other; however, I believe that this is only due to my cultural bias, and that a Wintu would have started from what for us is the other, from the gradual distinguishing of the self from society.

In our own culture, we are clear as to the boundaries of the self. In our commonly held unreflective view, the self is a distinct unit, something we can name and define. We know what is the self and what is not the self; and the distinction between the two is always the same. With the Wintu, the self has no strict bounds, is not named and is not, I believe, recognized as an entity. There are words which deal with the self alone. I do not include among them the *ni*: I, since this is completely dependent for its meaning on the conception of the self held by the speaker who is using it. There are, however, verbs dealing with being or activities and other experiences of the self. For example, we have *limelda*: ail-I. This clearly refers to the self. But what does *tutuhum limtcada*:[5] mother—objective *ail-tca-I*, or *sukuyum limtcada*: dog—objective *ail-tca-I* refer to? Which is self and which is other here? The phrases mean, in our terms: my mother is ill, or my dog is ill; but the Wintu is not referring to a distinct, related other, but rather to an other in which he is involved. Actually, this phrasing is used only when speaking of intimates; it is also possible—but I do not know how common—to say in so many words: my mother ails.

[1] D. D. Lee, 'Conceptual Implications of an Indian Language.' *Philosophy of Science*, 5:89-102, 1938.
[2] *Ibid;* and D. D. Lee, 'Linguistic Reflection of Wintu Thought.' *International Journal of American Linguistics*, 10:181-187, 1944.
[3] D. D. Lee, 'Categories of the Generic and the Particular in Wintu.' *American Anthropologist*, 46:362-369, 1944.
[4] D.D. Lee, 'Stylistic Use of the Negative in Wintu.' *International Journal of American Linguistics*, 12:79-81, 1946.
[5] Since this is not primarily a linguistic paper, I have taken liberties in the spelling of the Wintu words, in the interests of simplicity.

Our own linguistic usage through the years, reveals a conception of an increasingly assertive, active and even aggressive self, as well as of an increasingly delimited self. In Chaucer's English, we find the reflection of a way of thinking where events happened to the self much more often than our own usage implies. In Chaucer we find: 'it reweth *me*', 'thus dreamed *me*', '*melikes*' and '*himlikode*'; but we say now: *I* rue, *I* dream, *I* like. Not only do we think of ourselves as actors here, but we phrase this 'activity' as directed at a distinct other. When I say: I like him, I cast my statement into the subject-to-object-affected mold; I imply that I have done something to him. Actually, he may be totally ignorant of my liking and unaffected; only I myself am certainly and directly affected by it. Again, the so-called analytic and isolating trend in our language, actually separates the self from the encompassing situation. The delimitation of the self is reflected in our increasing analysis of holistic Anglo-Saxon terms referring to bodily acts. I *beckon* is becoming literary or at least cultivated; I *gape* is being replaced by phrases such as: with my mouth open. I say: *I* shake *my* fist, *I* bump *my* head; and how much is left of *me*, the self?

Our language implies not only that the self is narrowly delimited, but that it is also in control. *My* is the pronoun which we call possessive, whose distinguishing characteristic is that of possession or ownership, and possession in our culture means control: mine, to do with as I wish. And *my* is a word very frequently used. It is difficult to say what exactly is this self which is delimited and in control. We say: my time, my life—in the sense of *zoe* as well as of *bios*—my experience, my consciousness, my reason, my emotions, my identity. As far as the physical aspect is concerned, there seems to be a central point to which the *my* refers the various fragments. We say: I lift my foot, but there is no such relationship between hand and foot; I cannot say: my hand lifts its foot. The two are referred to the self; they are related only through the self and are both subordinate to the self. But the self, is not identified with the physical aspect of the individual. *I* am also in control of *my* body, which I dress, I adorn, I abuse.

When it comes to the non-physical aspects, we note a reflection of the dualism of mind and matter and the hierarchy which is a corollary of this. 'Passions' are considered lower: I *fall* in love, I *fall* into a passion or a rage. I delve into my unconscious, which is implicitly underneath; but I analyze my conscious, where I do not need to excavate, since it is on my level. I lose and recover my consciousness or my reason; I never *fall* into consciousness or reason. I control my emotions, but I do not control my consciousness or reason. Neither do I control my will; I exercise it. The

46

self is most nearly identified with consciousness and reason and will; and in our culture, reason and will power and consciousness—particularly self-consciousness—spell mastery and control. So here, too, we find the implication that the self is in control of the other.

In Wintu, there is no such fragmenting. When I asked my informant Sadie Marsh what the word for *body* was, she said *kot Wintu*, the whole person. To the Wintu a person is holistic; he is psychosomatic, but without the suggestion of synthesis which this term holds. They have no word for body or corpse, and the so-called parts of the body are aspects or locations. Neither do they have a word for the self. In English, the word has a long history; and the compounds *myself* and *yourself* were in use by the fourteenth century. The Wintu language does not show the presence of a concept of an established separate self; but the Wintu can emphasize one 'self', and through the use of grammatical devices he can distinguish an individual at will. The suffix *'a* added to *pi*: he, means *he himself*; *yoken* added to *pi* means *he alone*. The suffix *ken*, added to a name or other noun emphasizes the individual referred to in contrast to all other individuals who have been included in the expectation. For example, *Sadieken hina* means: *Sadie-of-all-those-expected has-come.*

A study of the grammatical expression of identity, relationship and otherness, shows that the Wintu conceive of the self not as strictly delimited or defined, but as a concentration, at most, which gradually fades and gives place to the other. Most of what is other for us, is for the Wintu completely or partially or upon occasion, identified with the self. For example, the Wintu do not use *and* when referring to individuals who are, or live or act together. Instead of analyzing the *we* into: *John and I*, they say *John we*, using the John as a specification. Only when two individuals who are not already in relatedness are brought together, is the *and* used. Quite often relatives are referred to in terms of the plural of togetherness. For example: *sohapulel pel*: *sibling—*(verb)*—together the-two*: he and his sister; *sedet pel putahtchupulel bos*: *coyote they-two grandmother-together lived; yoqupulel*: *wash together* or *wash each other*. Notice that except for the *soha*, the relationship presented is inherently one-directional, so that the togetherness is viewed from one point of view. In the example representing an activity, the *pulel* can be seen as referring to mutuality; but I think that this is a concept introduced from our own culture. In most cases what we find is spatial and temporal concurrence; for example: *ilawi watchupurebinte*: *the babies are (all) crying together* (according to my hearing); *bolpurun piterum tchuhpure*: *drink-together-while they gambled-together.*

47

As with us, the being or existence of the self and activities of the self in process, are expressed as identical with the self; though our own usage, which separates the person from the verb implies some separation. So in *I go*, the ego is separated from its own activity, *go*. The Wintu says *harada*: *I go* or *we go*, in one unanalyzed word, and uses *ni* (I) or *niterum* (we) only if he wishes to, by way of clarification or denotation. He uses exactly the same form when he refers to a part of the body, or even to the clothing which he has on; for example, *I-go-weak legs*: *my legs are growing weak*. A Wintu will say: *I-am-red-face*, or *face-I-am-red*, where face refers to place or aspect of the whole person. He will say: *you-are-ripped-clothes*, or *you-are-pretty-dress striped*; and: *nose-run-I* or *arm-broke-I*. Unlike us, a Wintu self is identical with the parts of his body and is not related to them as other, so long as they are physically part of him. But when a hair has fallen off his head, it as *his* hair, when a heart has been plucked out of a man it is *his* heart, when a man has cut off his arm it is *his* arm; and when a woman is folding her dress it is *her* dress. When they are physically separated, they are related to him.

When a Wintu performs an act whose consequences revert upon himself, he uses a suffix, *-na*. He phrases holistically, what we phrase in terms of reversion to the self as a grammatical object. We say, *I feel* (cold) and, *I feel myself* (with my hands); i.e., *I* is stated as separate from the self. The Wintu says *muteda*, *I-feel*, and *mutnada*: *I-feel-myself*.

I now come to forms which I find very difficult to describe and present. There is the suffix of the form which I quoted above: *limtcada*: (my child) *ail-tca-I*. It probably can be most adequately translated here in the Irish English idiom: *my mother got sick on me*; but the Wintu implies a greater degree of involvement, since the verb is given in the first person, the self, not the person of the other. The suffix gives a definitive cast or an active cast to an otherwise vague or merely passive (i.e., non-participating and non-active) verb. For example, it may make a transitive out of an intransitive verb, or may delimit an activity into one act. I think that what we call transitivity is for the Wintu a kind of reference or a delimitation of the act; and that is why the *tca* can be used for (what is for us) such a variety of purposes. For example, the Wintu says *semdaqalda*: *hand-I-got-scorched* and *bas daqtcada*: *food I-scorched*; or is it: *I got scorched* in reference to my food, with the food conceived as one degree more separate from the self than the hand, which is a part of the self? With the same suffix, the Wintu also changes *lipe*, as in: *mem lipeda*: *water thirst-I*, into *liptchada*, as in: *tutuhum liptcada*: *mamma thirst-tca-I, my mother is thirsty*.

There are two other suffixes, which also imply a certain degree of otherness in which the individual participates coordinately, or in which he is otherwise involved. The suffix *ma* represents thinking which runs counter to our own, and was very difficult for me to understand. For a long time I considered it a causative; *ba*, for example, I translated as *to eat*, and *bama* as to *feed, to cause to eat; peru* means *to swallow* and *peruma*: to *fish with bait; taqiq* means *to hurt* and *taqiqmabinte* means *she made me hurt* (I feel). This was all clearly causative. However, the weight of the accumulated obscure exceptions finally overpowered my rule. For example, I found phrases such as the following:

*applum hesihamada: apples pithy-ma-am.* Yet I have not caused my apples to be pithy; in fact, Sadie, who said this, had just bought the apples.

*hlalmas nis ibesken: stink me you-are:* (*hlal* means to stink and *mas* is the second person of *ma*) *you think that I stink.*

*kot bahlmastot . . . tchuqpure: all menstruating-for-the-first-time-ma-these . . . helped together;* i.e., all the relatives of the pubescent girl helped; this was said of the male relatives of the pubescent girl.

To make the *ma* comprehensible to members of our society, we have to translate it either as a causative or as adverb-forming. For example, *tchala* means *to be good* or *nice*, and *tchaluma* means *to do well* or *do carefully; tcaluma il* means *be careful!* Then, *tepumas tchalumatchupumada:* (my) *garden nicely grow-ma-am*, may be translated as: I made my garden grow nicely, or: I am doing well in respect to my garden. Primary in the *ma* is the implication of involvement or participation; this may be interpreted by us as a continuity of participation in another state or act (i.e., as an adverb), or as manipulative. I cannot tell whether these different meanings are present for the Wintu; Sadie told me that *tchupumada* did not necessarily imply that I was taking care of my garden. I think the implication of control is absent from the suffix.

The other suffix, *il*, also appears to express aggressive action, at first encounter. In our own phrasing, whereas *ma* could be manipulative (to get him to do), *il* would be out and out aggressive; *il* would be translated as to do to. So, *woi* means *to come*, and *iweril*, *to bring; pile* means *to wind*, and *hunpilewil* means *bound him up*. But then we also have: *put tupuwilda: him-weed-il-I*. This means: *I weeded with him*. All similar situations which, wherever possible, we express as aggressive acts, are given as coordinate relationships among the Wintu. The term for what is to us possession or ownership is formed by means of this suffix, from the three kinds of *to be*: in a standing, sitting or lying position. *I have a basket* means really *I live with* or *I sit with a basket*, and is expressed with the same form as that used to say: I live with my grandmother, or I am married (to Harry). The term *sukil* which I translated at first as to rule, actually means, to *be-with-in-a-standing-position*, and expresses the true democracy of the Wintu where a chief stood-with his people.

When the *il* is used as a suffix to a verb, the grammatical object of the verb is particularized for the occasion, and all pronouns and adjectives referring to it are given special suffixes reflective of the coordinate relationship.[1]

There is another suffix, *me*, which also we would translate as transitivizing; and this, I think, even the Wintu would consider as expressive of control, or at least of separation from the self. A man speaking of a man's possessions, in telling a myth, used the *il and* the whole range of particularizing suffixes; a woman telling the same myth, using the same verbs used the *me* instead and left the grammatical object and its attributes in its original generic form. I think the *me* does not contain the respect which is present in the *il;* and its appearance in my texts is not frequent.[2]

The Wintu conception of the self then differs from our own in that it contains the total person and the activities of all its aspects, and in that it fades out gradually and without distinct demarcation. It is not clearly opposed to the other, neither is it clearly identical with or incorporated in the other. In most occasions it participates to some extent in the other, and is coordinate with the other; where we see a one way relationship from self to other, an assertion of the self upon the other, the Wintu see a togetherness, with, at most, a stressed point of view. For example, the phrase I quoted above: *put tupuwilda, I weeded with him,* happens to start with the self; it might have been: *nis tupuwil: he weeded with me.*

This gradually fading involvement of the self in the other can be seen also in the use of the three relational pronouns which are translated in English as *my*. The *neto* refers to objects which I would not hesitate to refer to in terms of the distant or aggressive *me*, and which are spoken of in their generic form. *Netomen* is used for objects for which I am also prepared to use *il*. No *my*, of course, is used for body parts, since these are identical with and not related to the person. Finally, *net* is used for close relatives as well as acts and states of the self.[3] When referring to close relatives, the *net* is inseparable from the kinship term. Even when referring to an unspecified father, where we would say 'the

---

[1] 'Categories of the Generic and the Particular in Wintu.' *op cit.*
[2] *Ibid;* and 'Linguistic Reflection of Wintu Thought.' *op. cit.*
[3] D. D. Lee, 'The Place of Kinship Terms in Wintu Speech.' *American Anthropologist,* 42:604-616, 1940.

father' the Wintu says his-father (or her-father).[1] When speaking of *my act* or *my liking* or *my death* or *my destination*, the Wintu separates the *my* from the following word. As I can say *I act* as well as *my act*, so I can also say, *I-younger-sister: I have a younger sister*; and *I-mother: I have a mother* as well as *my fathered: he who has been made into a father by me*, i.e., through my being born. The relatives of this intimate group are treated in the same way as one's acts or state of being.

Linguistic analysis further shows us a different relationship between the self and reality in general from that which is basic to our own culture. The Wintu never asserts the truth as absolute, as we do when we say *it is*. In one of the common stories about the German, the Frenchman and the Englishman, the first two, pointing to bread, say, 'I call it Brot', and 'I call it pain'; but the Englishman says, 'I call it bread and it *is* bread. 'The Wintu never say it *is* bread. They say, 'It looks-to-me-bread' or 'It feels-to-me bread' or 'I-have-heard-it-to-be bread' or 'I-infer-from-evidence-that-it-is bread' or 'I-think-it-to-be-bread,' or, vaguely and timelessly, 'according-to-my-experience-be bread'.[2] The statement is made about the third person, the bread, but with the implication that its validity is limited by the specified experience of the speaker.

For us, that which we sense or know according to man-made rules of logic is; and that which is beyond my apprehension, beyond my sensing or cognition, is fiction. The self is the measure of all things. Art and metaphysics and religious experience are barely tolerated on the fringes of our culture. When the fairy godfather first appeared in the Barnaby cartoon, he left a trail of cigar ashes by way of visual proof of his visit. Mysticism is now a bad word among the intellectuals, and is defined negatively as loss of self. No one in ecstasy is taken seriously, until he comes to his senses. Only when the self is logically and cognitively in control, is experience valid, and only that which is ultimately open to such experience is true. To the Wintu, the experience of the self must be always documented and can be questioned. It is given always through a special derivative stem, usually with a variety of suffixes which make reference to the source of information. The original, primary form of the stem is used to point to not experienced, unquestioned reality, to natural necessity. Only with the first of these stems does he use assertive suffixes; but here he asserts, not truth, but experience—perception, cognition, reflection, inference—which is open to question, which is limited by his being, and which need not correspond with the truth.

---

[1] It may be of significance here that the terms referring to these relatives are classified not with the nouns, but with the relational words such as other-one, this-one, everyone, which. I believe this was also the case in Indo-European, since such words have the same suffix; for example, father, sister, kinder, rather, either, other.
[2] 'Conceptual Implications of an Indian Language.' *op. cit.*

In other ways, also, we find that with the Wintu the universe is not centered in the self, as it is with us. Take, for example, the term which we used for the individual about whom we are going to speak: ego: I. If the anthropologist wants to make a kinship chart, he starts with ego. If I conjugate, I start with *I run*, and having started with it, I naturally call it the first person; and rightly so, since, in present day English, the third person with its -s suffix is derivative. In Wintu, on the other hand, the third person is primary, and the first is derived. The third person may be represented by the simple stem of experience; or, if a suffix is used, this occurs in the simple stem. The first person is formed derivatively, through suffixation of -da to the simple stem or to the suffix.[1]

There is reason to believe, furthermore, that Wintu words are formed on the basis of an outward orientation. They are based on observation, rather than on the kineasthetic experience of the self, or on introspection.[2] Take, for instance, the word for *tick, terus*. It is derived from *tira: to pound to a pulp*. This would mean that *tira* is not concerned with the pounding experience of the self, or with the experience of being pounded, but rather with the shape of the resulting mass. The word for *wade*—fast disappearing among the bilingual Wintu means: *to-make-a-great-splashing-noise*. The word *tsiqoha: to-disappear-all-at-once*, is derived from the stem of *tsiqtca*, which means *to be put through a sieve*; that is, to sieve is concerned merely with the observed result of the sieving.

In myths, people are described in terms of the spatial dimension of their activities, observationally. Extremely rarely is there a statement that might be called introspective; such as 'she was furious', or 'he was happy'; and even here, I am not sure that this is not an observer's statement. The songs the Wintu call love songs refer not at all to the sensations or emotions of love, though they do convey love to us. For example:

> From-Hawk's-scratch-gap
> Downhill-northward-before-you-go
> Oh, look-back-at-me.

The sleeping place which you and I hollowed out will remain forever.

I have recorded a tale which my informant called a love story. It describes the pursuit of a man by two women who were in love with him. I quote a sample of the story:

---

[1] I do not discuss the second person, because I do not understand the significance of its form. It is formed, not with the usual verbal stem, but with the nominal form of this stem; to this is suffixed the -ken which it singles out, emphasizes, or may even be said to oppose. At other times, also, the second person is treated completely differently from the other two; the warning suffix is -kedi and -kida for the third and first persons, and -ken for the second; -leso: before (he does) perforce, is the same for the first person, but -menso for the second. [2] 'Conceptual Implications of an Indian Language.' op cit.; and D. D. Lee, 'The Linguistic Aspect of Wintu Acculturation.' American Anthropologist, 45:435-440, 1943.

They went to the east side of the house, they went around to the east side, and after that they went up the hill to the north, following him running. They went northward at a running pace over the north flat, wishing to see the man who had gone down the hill northward (the word for wish also means to try). And the man was not there but there lay his tracks going forward. And they ran, they went at a running pace, they went rapidly. And at the South-slope-climb, when they came in full view of the north, they looked northward but they did not see him.

The Wintu use of *left* and *right,* as compared with ours, shows again the difference in orientation. When we go for a walk, the hills are to our right, the river to our left; when we return, the hills change and the river, while we remain the same, since we are the pivot, the focus. Now the hills have pivoted to the left of me. This has been English practice for many years, since at least the fourteenth century. To the Wintu, the terms left and right refer to inextricable aspects of his body, and are very rarely used. I think that only once the term left occurs in my texts, referring to a left-handed mythical hero; I cannot remember any occurrence of the term for right. When the Wintu goes up the river, the hills are to the west, the river to the east; and a mosquito bites him on the west arm. When he returns, the hills are still to the west, but, when he scratches his mosquito bite, he scratches his east arm. The geography has remained unchanged, and the self has had to be reoriented in relation to it.

I said in the beginning of this essay that I should have written from society as the starting point, or at any rate from what we consider the not-self. I came to this conclusion partly on the basis of the material which I have presented here, partly through my experience in recording an autobiography. When I asked Sadie Marsh for her autobiography, she told me a story about her first husband, based on hearsay. When I insisted on her own life history, she told me a story which she called, 'my story'. The first three quarters of this, approximately, are occupied with the lives of her grandfather, her uncle and her mother before her birth; finally, she reaches the point where she was 'that which was in my mother's womb', and from then on she speaks of herself, also.

In conclusion, I should like to state that the two different conceptions of the self need not be regarded as mutually contradictory. I believe that they can refer to the same absolute truth, and can be said to give us clues to this truth.

*Dorothy Lee*

The author of *Tristram Shandy* is distinguished among the novelists of his day for having avoided, in large measure, an outward apparent fiction in favour of an inward fiction. The best influences of philosophy play over his writing. If he did not with Berkeley think the world was all *ideal*, he did with Locke suppose it was all *idea*. With his very liquid inkwell he sets himself up in those black and green areas of the mind where Uncle Toby plays green games in green shades and Mr. Shandy has very black thoughts. To underline the shadowy darkness,—at once emotional and imaginative,—a Negro girl will come for a moment to whisk away black flies with a white feather duster. Here is impressionism, with the black race finding a new necessity and beauty in a psychological literature. Paris, with its nine hundred streets, is entered by candlelight.

In *Tristram Shandy* we are sitting beside a fireplace in the room of the mind, among candles and lanterns,—retired from business, in a state of cultivated inaction. The battlefields of Flanders have been reduced to the proportions of a bowling green. All Europe is becoming a small story, a map, a marrow pea. We hear the 'thee' and 'thou' of Ellian intimacy, and the silence of a sect can in rare moments weave 'dreams of midnight secrecy into the brain'.

Inside these brains of Sterne's fiction we meet occasionally a glassy French lady who dangles her toes, like a tadpole, in delicious Borrian juices. She is called the Soul. She has been surprised by intruders carrying Momus spyglasses. Sometimes she retires into a 'sweet secession' of sleep. One of her swimming companions is Curiosity, a nymph of psychic proportions blown in by a gale from a poem of Alexander Pope. But inside this common mind of Sterne's characters we are seeing much too little of this Cartesian lady and her nice attendants. Instead we are more literally and more constantly in the somewhat less beautiful company of the Imagination. Sterne's purposes as the novelist of *Tristram Shandy* were multiple. But surely it was a major part of his intention to illuminate man's imagination.

In *Tristram* Sterne approached this area with the chief assistance of the concept of associated ideas. You can hear the mind opening and shutting, like the windows and doors of Shandy Hall, with the clickings of association. Sterne's Devil himself is a part of an inward association world. He is a figure who sets himself up in the dark highways of the mind, there to manipulate the association sequence. Frequently he jumps astride the imagination as it comes rushing down its muddy lanes. As a psychological novel *Tristram Shandy* attempts to describe the imagination in the context of associationism. For all intents and purposes, Sterne is here creating the literature of association. This art, starting now, will widen into the poetry of Wordsworth and Keats: it will touch much autobiographical writing in the nineteenth century: and it will show itself abundantly in the poetry and fiction of our time.

Immediately in *Tristram* Sterne realizes that inward emotional intimacy which will separate associational literature from outward ethical attitudes. He finds too the poetry of his new world. But further he gives a dominant cast to the literature of association which is very much of a guide into the reading of any titles in this family, be it *The Prelude* or the *Remembrance of Things Past*.

If we submit ourselves properly to this novel, we shall feel that this associative imagination is always moving backwards, even as the story of Tristram works backwards into his own beginnings in the life of his parents and home. The associative imagination is the imagination of personal memory and of popular memory too. The past is pouring over present images like an old bearded waterfall. 'There is', says Sterne, 'but a certain degree of perfection in every thing.' Nothing has a single purity, in spite of a laundered cleanliness in the object. There is a constant intrusion of past upon present. The small hero is a patchwork of the older personalities of the fireside. And the fireside is feathered and thatched with a larger encrusted memory. Uncle Toby's blush goes back sixty years, and with a word all Picardy opens inside his memory. Whiskers suggest a story out of the kingdom of Navarre, and noses revert to old Strasburg. The name Tristram itself echoes the science of ancient Egypt and the sorrows of Ireland. The tombs of Auxerre are opened. Each word, each image in the Shandean screen is saturated with its implication in an historical continuum. The non-associational fiction around Sterne can hardly offer a comparable historical sense. Indeed such surrounding fiction would seem to be set in a present science, with all the tones of optimism flowing from the eighteenth-century view of the natural world. *Tom Jones* represents such fiction.

It is particularly the memory of Europe which Sterne allows to drench the objects of the reclining Shandean field. Sterne was the least insular of the novelists of his age, in that sense which is of importance. In incorporating the tradition of Europe in his fiction, he has used the less formal aspects of its culture, avoiding a Europe of Stoic epistles in favour of a Europe of legend and dream, of tales and naughty stories, of scholarship prophetically devoted to a folk tradition. It is a vulgar verbal stream, with its own essential folk symbolism as of a circus, which is allowed to wash over the garments, the Montero caps, the Turkish pipes of Shandy Hall. As we see Sterne rushing down the rapid Rhone, snatching wild grapes from the vineyards, we are reminded of the degree to which English poets and writers, affected perhaps by the rise of associationism, will now integrate themselves into the landscape and history of Europe. Boswell, Wordsworth and Byron will all in their different ways personally exploit the scene of Europe, and in each case we are aware of an importance added to their language as their words took on continental associations.

The associative imagination effects another large pattern in *Tristram*, which is the proper accompaniment of the historical matter of this novel. Repeatedly we see the individual being carried away rapidly on a hobby-horse, for which passing words and images have provided rising stirrups. They start from their chairs and ride. 'Say no more!' says Uncle Toby, as he takes off. Sterne is magnificent in picturing possessed persons, as groups as well as individuals. He shows whole villages like Strasburg, whole kingdoms like Navarre, mounting their horses and riding. The readers of *Tristram* are all too conscious of these equestrian personalities who ride palfreys and pads and jades and filly-follys and young mettlesome tits, that scour and scamper and trot and frisk and jerk, and squirt and gallop and curvet, and jump and rear and bound. But these beasts are still but stationary hobby-horses,—something, Sterne observes, to amuse an Englishman who can't go out-of-doors. There is no forward motion. There is rather a backward motion, and a solitary one, into those set imaginative habits and prejudices which were, many of them, drunk in with the mother's milk, or came with early education. And beyond these images lie the pools of personal fatigue. Sterne's wooden hobby-horses got their start very directly from Locke's chapter on the association of ideas, where, again without gloom, imaginative habit and prepossession are marked out.

Everywhere in *Tristram*, among textures sometimes misleading, we find a kind of determinism. The associative imagination is not quite a free imagination, it would appear. Sterne's chain of being was very literally a chain, and Mr. Shandy wore it like a Job, feeling that a retrograde planet hung over his unfortunate house, feeling the great 'imposition laid upon our nature'. The star of the mind receives association pressures at each point, from Europe and from everywhere. Association is indeed the mental counterpart of the law of gravity. The pressure affects Sterne's prose in an interesting way towards the end of the novel, where we see it hardly refraining from the last associative act,—the act of rhyme. It is accepting, as it were, the links of rhyme laid down by the past.

The reader of *Tristram* may come to feel that the associative imagination, as well as moving backwards, is perhaps always moving downwards towards a determined universal symbolism. This is a matter lying much deeper in this first novel about 'my father' than this paper will attempt to venture. It may be mentioned that Sterne does hint that Europe is on the point of accepting a universal symbolism. And he notes the storm warnings in that Navarrian title, the Curate of d'Estella's book on the dangers of accessory ideas.

Sterne effects hard aesthetic ways in *Tristram* to symbolize these determined views of life. He may be said to have developed the obsessive image, which has had such wide acceptance in subsequent literature. Such an obsessive image is the long-arrested gesture, as when Mr. Shandy lies for fifty pages face down on a bed, like one of Keats' fallen gods of time,—or when he stands for nearly as long on a landing. In the latter situation Sterne remarks that a critic (and here he jibes at formal art) is needed to move Shandy from the stairs. Obsessive images, such as the winds of Avignon, or white bears, or fish ponds, or eyes, or wheels, are approached with an epitomizing intensity that marks an innovation in symbolic style. The obsessive image is the stylistic counterpart of the fixed, wooden hobby-horse. The suspected word is a second evident mannerism in Sterne,—and through this device especially he enforces the sense of historical destinies. Every word that comes before us has a past, a shadow. Often its poor head is bruised and black. To intensify suspicion and implication, Sterne will employ the riddling phrase, the puzzling question: 'I go by water', 'And who are you?' Or he will hang up asterisks as lights in his text. These literary ways with images and words underline a story of limiting habit and historical imprint. Since an important relation of *Tristram* to *Hamlet* was clearly intended by Sterne, we might suppose that Sterne read back into *Hamlet* the language of association, and he may too have seen in this play the art-forms association suggests. The 'blistered word' is very much a part of the drama of *Hamlet*. The real burial of Ophelia is well anticipated by a funeral procession of language, the inky hearse holding Ophelia's own last garbled words. And Hamlet, who both talks about and rides hobby-horses, has a way of whirling around the 'obsessive image'. In this drama of Shakespeare, which explores the recessive spirit, Sterne may very properly have found literary manners for associational writing.

In all that *Tristram* is as a novel, in its matters and tone and backward manners, we come finally to feel history, the past, and therewith a certain determinism. This is the genealogical vision which came to Sterne through the exercise and understanding of the associative imagination. It is not too much to say that he went beyond his master Locke in realizing the historical implications of association philosophy.

His brilliant, and obviously timely, perceptions are supported by another writing of the 1760's, which was privately directing literature along the ways of association. I refer to the *Private Papers* of James Boswell, the more intimate of which may properly be called studies in the imagination. Boswell's instrument in the analysis of his imagination was, as in Sterne's case, the Lockian concept of the association of ideas. In watching himself closely as he did, Boswell was very conscious of the association possibilities in dress and music. A fancy-dress ball was accordingly the proper moment for James Boswell to do his most intensive self-study. A Domino of white with red ribbands, loaned him for a dance at the German court of Saxe-Gotha, transferred him immediately to Spain, while a Scots country dance at the court of Dessau set going a curious mixture of German and Caledonian ideas. 'I had', he notes, 'just the sensations as when a Boy at Culross, and Valleyfield. I find it is no impossible Matter to be just what one has formerly been.' Again, as in Sterne, the currents of association were always carrying him back in time. An old French tune sung at an inn, the chateau of Colombier, a gloomy Sunday in Switzerland, moved him ever backwards to Scotland, to home, and to the dominant, and thoroughly unpleasant, parent image. The associationism of Hazlitt, we observe, took a similar, though pleasant, parental direction. For Boswell the chains went further back in time. To one of his numerous prospective fathers-in-law, he wrote: 'I know not by what association of ideas, the rich pastures where your Cows graze appear to me like the fields of the Pious Patriarchs.'—'Can preexistence be true?', he asks himself elsewhere when confronted with strong elements of the past in his imagination. The importance of the Boswell Papers to the history of association literature makes their publication in our time a literary event. Boswell's associationism likewise featured a hobby-horse,— the gloom to which his imagination continually reverted. Over the oak forests of Germany sound the noble horns of hunting parties, red and blue, which this young associationist joined in an effort to outride his black hobby-horse.

Boswell and Sterne nicely illustrate the 'fixities and definites' which Coleridge was later, in the *Biographia Literaria*, to assign to the school of association. As well as offering such illustration, they also present the picture of an escape from associationism which anticipates Coleridge's own experience. Both Boswell and Sterne went beyond the reference of association to achieve imaginative work which must be spoken of in different terms. The well-composed conversation pieces of the *Life of Johnson*, and the splendid, still scenes of *A Sentimental Journey* belong to an imagination to which the concept of association cannot be felt to be central. In Boswell's case the progress out of association was a slow and painful business. For Sterne the transition was more simply intellectual, and it would appear to have been both cheerfully and quickly achieved.

*Kenneth MacLean*

In the Spring of this year, an interdisciplinary seminar on Culture and Communication from the departments of Anthropology, English, Political Economy, Psychology and Town Planning at the University of Toronto, conducted the following experiment in cooperation with the Canadian Broadcasting Corporation:

One hundred and thirty-six students from the Second Year General Course, on the basis of their over-all academic standing of the previous year, were divided into four equal groups who either (1) heard and saw a lecture delivered in a television studio, (2) heard and saw this same lecture on a television screen, (3) heard it over the radio, or (4) read it in manuscript. Thus there were, in the CBC studios, four controlled groups who simultaneously received a single lecture and then immediately wrote an identical examination to test both understanding and retention of content. Later the experiment was repeated, using three similar groups from the Second Year General Course. This time the same lecture was (1) delivered in a classroom, (2) presented as a film in a small theatre (using the television kinescope of the first lecture), and (3) again read in manuscript. The actual mechanics of the experiment were relatively simple, but the problem of writing the script for the lecture lead us to a consideration of the different resources and limitations of various dramatic forms.

It immediately became apparent that no matter how the script was written and the show produced, it would be slanted in various ways for and against each of the media involved; no show could be produced which did not contain these biases, and the only real common denominator would be the simultaneity of presentation. It was decided not to exploit the full resources of any one medium, but to try to chart a middle-of-the-road course between all of them. In short, the show was to be equally adapted for each of the media, or more accurately, to belong to none of them. The alternative, of taking a single theme and writing a separate show for each medium, we plan to attempt at a later date.

The lecture which was finally produced dealt with linguistic codifications of reality and metaphysical concepts underlying grammatical systems. It was chosen because it concerned a field in which few of any students could be expected to have prior knowledge, and moreover it offered opportunities for the use of body movements, especially hand gestures. The cameras moved throughout the lecture, and close-ups were taken when facial expressions and hand movements were particularly relevant. No other visual aids were used, nor were shots taken of the audience while the lecture was in progress. Instead, the cameras simply focused on the speaker for twenty-seven minutes.

Now an audience can give their attention to a man actually speaking to them for that length of time; but to look at the static picture of the same man for twenty-seven minutes would be an intolerable strain. So the cameras never stood still. It then became the problem of the television producer to decide at what point on the screen, at every minute, the eyes of the audience were to be directed. The audience was, in fact, looking at the picture—though they did not realize it—through the eyes of the producer. They saw what he made the cameras see. The experience was thus filtered first through his mind, and that part of it which he controlled, he structured. The greater his success in organizing it, the greater was the audience's illusion of being eye-witnesses of an event actually taking place. Frequent discussions therefore were held with the producer, Mr. Sydney Newman, in which we accepted nearly all of his suggestions, with one exception. That exception arose from the fact that his first concern was to produce the best possible television show, but the one we envisaged, and which was actually produced, sacrificed some of the resources of television in order to remain as neutral as possible. We are especially grateful to Mr. Newman for letting us experiment in this way, particularly since, had the show been a failure, he would have been held responsible.

61

The first difference we found between a classroom and a television lecture was the brevity of the latter. The classroom lecture, if not ideally, at least in practice, sets a slower pace. It is verbose and repetitive; it allows for greater elaboration and permits the lecturer to take up several *related* points. The television show, however, is stripped right down; there is less time for qualifications or alternative interpretations, and only time enough for *one* point. (Into twenty-seven minutes we put the meat of a two-hour classroom lecture.) The ideal television speaker states his point and then brings out different facets of it by a variety of illustrations. But the classroom lecturer is less subtle and, to the agony of the better students, explicitly repeats and repeats his identical points in the hope that ultimately no student will miss them.

The next major difference noted was the abstracting role of television. Selectivity in print and radio are obvious enough, but we are less conscious of it in television, perhaps because of television's greater realism.[1]

As in a movie theatre, only the screen is illuminated, and on it, only points of immediate relevance are portrayed; everything else is eliminated. Moreover, it is important that what you see not detract from what you hear, and vice versa. Sight and sound are not merely coordinated here; they become a single, unique language which proceeds at a different pace than radio. This became apparent first when the script, timed for radio, proved a fifth too long for television; another script might have been too short. Similarly, what was satisfactory over television sounded slow and disjointed over radio. Dr. Birdwhistell's article makes clear why this was so: each employs a separate language—one purely oral, the other verbal and kinesic, combined with situational data. The use of visual aids and body movements on television not only makes possible the elimination of certain words, but requires a unique script. The ideal radio broadcast, on the other hand, is written otherwise and delivery stresses pitch and intonation to make up for the absence of visual data. That flat, broken speech in 'sidewalk interviews' is the speech of a person untrained in radio delivery.

Television is designed for an audience of two or three; film for a crowd. The drive-in theatre leaves one with a feeling of isolation, of lacking the anonymity and passivity one associates with cinema. Moreover, the timing, particularly for jokes, is too slow.

---

[1] K. and G. L. Lang (*American Sociological Review*, 18:1) contrast the recorded experience of thirty-one participant observers who watched the 'MacArthur Day' parade in Chicago with the picture of this event given over television. The general impression on the screen was of a landslide effect of national indignation at MacArthur's abrupt dismissal that bordered on mass hysteria. This effect was achieved by editing the visual field and by a commentary that bore little relation to observable fact. Here, as in all the new media, the dramatic was not only stressed but in a sense, created.

In one sense, television is more intimate than a lecture delivered to a large audience. The cameras lead the spectator from a total view to a close-up, and back again, creating a dynamic picture. And the speaker appears to be looking at, and speaking directly to, the individual listener; even when he turns to one side or looks down, he does so as if in personal conversation with the listener. In this experiment it proved necessary to eliminate the results of the studio group for several reasons, the most important of which concerned this point. In the studio the lecturer was forced to address the cameras and thus to ignore the students. He was on a raised platform and literally spoke over their heads. Some of the students, in an effort to establish contact with him, turned in their seats and watched the show on a monitor set in the studio.

Face-to-face discourse is not as selective as television; it comes closer to communicating an unabridged situation than any other medium and involves the direct give and take of a dynamic relationship. Of course, there can be personal involvement in the other media. When Richardson's *Pamela* was serialized in 1741, it aroused such interest that in one English town, upon receipt of the last installment, the church bell announced that virtue had been rewarded. Radio stations have reported receiving quantities of baby clothes and bassinets when, in a soap opera, a heroine had a baby. BBC and *News Chronicle* report cases of women viewers who kneel before their television sets to kiss male announcers good night. However, only in personal conversation is there genuine participation and satisfactory reciprocity. Whether this means it's more convincing, I do not know.

I was recently told a story about a Polish couple who, though long resident in Toronto, retained many of the customs of their homeland. Their son despaired of ever getting his father to buy a suit cut in style or of the mother ever taking an interest in Canadian life. Then he bought them a television set and in a matter of months a major change took place. One evening the mother remarked that 'Edith Piaf is the latest thing on Broadway' and the father appeared in 'the kind of suit executives wear on television'. For years the father had passed this same suit in store windows and seen it both in advertisements and on living men, but not until he saw it on television did it become meaningful. I think this same statement goes for all media: each offers a unique presentation of reality which when new has a freshness and clarity that is extraordinarily powerful.

When T. S. Eliot adapted *Murder in the Cathedral* for film, he noted a difference in realism between cinema and stage:

The first and most obvious difference, I found, was that the cinema

63

(even where fantasy is introduced) is much more realistic than the stage. Especially in an historical picture, the setting, the costume, and the way of life represented have to be accurate. Even a minor anachronism is intolerable. On the stage much can be overlooked or forgiven; and indeed, an excessive care for accuracy of historical detail can become burdensome and distracting. In watching a stage performance, the member of the audience is in direct contact with the actor, is always conscious that he is looking at a stage and listening to an actor playing a part. In looking at a film, we are much more passive; as audience, we contribute less. We are seized with the illusion that we are observing an actual event, or at least a series of photographs of the actual event; and nothing must be allowed to break this illusion. Hence the precise attention to detail. . . .

Eliot is referring to *visual* realism, not subject matter. All the characters in *The Loon's Necklace*, for example, are Northwest Coast Indian masks. This is pure cinema; it could only be done on film. It stresses fantasy by exploiting that which is unique to film.

I doubt if the same can be said of television. Just what television is, is hard to say; it has yet to find itself and today fills in with older media: movies, plays, puppet shows, forums, lectures. But one unique and obvious feature is its realistic drama. The attractive feature of televised political conventions and investigations comes in part from the fact that cameras do not focus on speakers, but on persons spoken to or about; the audience *hears* the accuser but *watches* the accused. They watch the trembling hands of the big-town crook. This is real drama, in process, with the outcome uncertain. Books and movies can only pretend uncertainty, but television captures this vital aspect of experience. Seen on television, the fire in the 1952 Democratic Convention threatened briefly to become a conflagration; seen on a newsreal, it was history, without potentiality.

Precisely because the other media differ from television in both approach and content, the absence of this element of uncertainty is not necessarily a handicap to them. Thus it is clear from the beginning that Hamlet is a doomed man, but far from detracting in interest, this heightens the sense of tragedy.

Now one of the results of the time-space duality which developed in Western culture from the Renaissance on, was a separation within the arts. Music, which created symbols in time, and graphic art, which created symbols in space, became separate pursuits, and men gifted in one rarely pursued the other. Dance and ritual, which inherently com-

64

bined them, fell in popularity. Only in drama did they remain united. It is significant that of the four new media, the three most recent are essentially dramatic media, particularly television which combines music and art, language and gesture, rhetoric and colour. They convey emotional tones, not merely 'information'. They do not, however, exercise the same freedom with time that the stage practices. An intricate plot, employing flash-backs, multiple perspective, and overlays, intelligible on the stage, might be completely mystifying on the screen. The audience has no time to think back, to establish relations between early hints and subsequent discoveries. The picture passes before the eyes too quickly; and there are no intervals in which to take stock of what has happened, and make conjectures of what is going to happen. The observer is in a more passive state, less interested in subtleties. Both television and film are nearer to narrative and depend much more upon the episodic. An intricate time construction can be done visually, but in fact rarely is. On stage Ophelia's death is described by three separate groups: one hears the announcement and watches the reactions simultaneously. On film the camera shows her drowned where 'a willow lies aslant a brook'.

It became apparent from differences such as these, that it was not simply a question of communicating a single idea over various media, but that a given type of idea or insight belongs primarily, though not exclusively, to one medium, and that it can be gained or communicated best through that medium.

Thus the format of the book favours lineal expression, for the argument runs like a thread from cover to cover: subject to verb to object, sentence to sentence, paragraph to paragraph, chapter to chapter, carefully structured from beginning to end. This is not true of drama, at least good drama, nor of good literature generally, which has always employed multi-perspective, but it is true of most books, particularly texts, histories, legal briefs and autobiographies. Events are arranged chronologically and hence, it is assumed, causally; relationship, not being, is valued. The book is ideally suited for discussing, say, evolution.

But the form of the new mass media favours discontinuity, not lineality. The newspaper format offers short, discreet articles which give important facts first and then taper off to incidental details which may, and often are, eliminated by the make-up man. The fact that reporters cannot control the length of articles means that in writing them, emphasis cannot be placed on structure, at least in the traditional sense, with the climax or conclusion at the end. The position and size of articles on the front page is determined by interest and importance, not content. Unrelated reports from Moscow, Sarawak, London and Ittipuk are juxtaposed;

time and space are destroyed and the *here* and the *now* are presented as a single gestalt. Such a format lends itself to simultaniety, not chronology or lineality. Items abstracted from a total situation are not arranged in causal sequence, but presented in association, as raw experience. Much the same may be said of the other new media. Both radio and television offer short, unrelated programs, interrupted between and within by commercials. I say 'interrupted', being myself an anachronism of book culture, but my children do not regard commercials as interruptions, as breaking continuity. They regard them rather as parts of a whole, and their reaction is neither one of annoyance nor indifference. The ideal news-broadcast has half a dozen speakers report from as many parts of the world on as many subjects.

In magazines, where a writer more frequently controls the length of his article, he can, if he wishes, organize it in the traditional style, but the majority do not. Moreover, the format as a whole opposes lineality. In *Life,* extremes are juxtaposed: space ships and prehistoric monsters, Flemish monasteries and dope addicts. This variety creates a sense of speed and urgency. One encounters, within a few pages, a riot in Teheran, a Hollywood marriage, the wonders of the Eisenhower administration, a two-headed calf, and a party on Jones beach, all sandwiched between advertisements. The eye takes in the page as a whole (readers may pretend this isn't so, but the success of advertising suggests it is), and the page—perhaps the whole magazine—becomes a single gestalt where association, though not causal, is often life-like.

In this rapid change in Western culture from an emphasis upon lineality to a presentation which is essentially magical—I use the word with explicit meaning—the new mass media have played a central role. Certainly in format they are attuned to non-lineal presentation, and some of the older media are being modified to fit it.

The role of museums is a case in point. Archeological and natural history museums came into existence in the second half of the 19th century to teach evolution. Ancient tools, for example, were arranged in unilinear sequence with the simplest, and allegedly oldest, at the bottom and the most complex at the top. Here was evidence that every layman could see and understand, more convincing than anything described in print. But after the argument had been won, and when doubts about the unilinear nature of evolution developed, this display technique was abandoned. For a while displays were built around themes (generally ones which dealt with production and distribution of commodities), but in spite of the enthusiasm with which such renovation was undertaken, it awakened little public interest. The solution lay, directors found, in turning museums into art cathedrals. The ideal museum was divided into two separate units: one for display, the other for laboratories and study collections. A gallery with a vaulted ceiling, light walls, a large, central statue of Buddha illuminated by shafts of descending light and surrounded by a few outstanding and artistically displayed pieces (often in the open and with only brief labels)—this was the type of gallery which brought crowds back into museums. Emphasis had shifted from relationship to being.

We were advised, when setting up this experiment, that television, being new and exciting, would command greater audience attention now than it might in later years. I think this is true. But print, the oldest mass medium, also enjoys an advantage: prestige. And the newer media are slighted, particularly in academic circles.

Dr. Chaytor's article on psychological differences between speech and print shows that each is a unique medium, and that print is not simply the visual recording of speech. Pitch and intonation are left to phrasing and punctuation; body movements are inferred or ignored; etc.[1] Edmund M. Morgan, Harvard Law Professor, writes:

> One who forms his opinion from the reading of any record alone is prone to err, because the printed page fails to produce the impression or convey the idea which the spoken word produced or conveyed. The writer has read charges to the jury which he had previously heard delivered, and has been amazed to see an oral deliverance which indicated a strong bias appear on the printed page as an ideally impartial exposition. He has seen an appellate court solemnly declare the testimony of a witness to be especially clear and convincing which the trial judge had orally characterized as the most abject perjury.

Technically, print leaves much to be desired as a communication form. Yet the remarkable thing is the achievements made with it, particularly in book form. Indeed, the influence of the book has been so great, that its limitations and resources have become, to a surprising degree, the limitations and resources of Western thought. This is particularly true of a university audience. Rigid verbal grammar, a product of literacy, is valued; rhetoric and gestures are avoided and left to unlettered evangelists, politicians and salesmen; the non-lineal argument is distrusted.

[1] F. N. Stanton (*The Journal of Applied Psychology*, 1934; summarized in *Sponsor*, 8:7) performed experiments with 160 students to determine which mode of transmitting fictitious advertising copy was more effective: print or radio. The oral copy was presented by loudspeaker without a program — no music or dialogue; the printed material, identical in content, was given without illustrations or display type. Two groups of eight ads each were used for both. Then the students were given recall, aided recall and recognition tests one day, seven days and twenty-one days after exposure for correct trade-name-commodity association. In all three tests for all three periods, the auditory method proved superior. 'When we consider that the college student is a trained reader, such an experiment with other persons may even show a greater difference in favor of audition for certain economic levels.'

It is not print which academics respect, but the book format with its bias toward lineality. Newspapers and magazines they regard as entertainment forms. But the book is associated with the Bible, culture, scholarship, law, science. It was the one means in the 19th century by which a poor man, cut off from the conversation of the leisure class, could become self-educated. Its relative permanence gives it an air of immortality: the written word embalming truth for posterity. Recently when it became apparent that populations such as India's might by-pass literacy and go directly to television, some academics were appalled; their reaction was reminiscent of that of the Russians in the United Nations who protested that Stone Age Melanesians would have to go first through the Bronze and Iron ages before they could accept modern civilization.

Our very concepts of mind and truth have, until recently, been inseparably associated with that portion of reality best communicated by print. *Coca Cola* can make any claim it wishes *pictorially*, but what it says in *print* must conform with Federal law. Whether this means that print, precisely because it is taken seriously and critically examined, is therefore more effective, I do not know.

Print enjoys an intrinsic advantage of greater importance: the reader controls exposure. He reads when he pleases, pauses when he wishes, and repeats or skips sections at will. Of all the advantages enjoyed by each of the media, I think this is the most significant.

THE SCRIPT

The script was re-written five times in an effort to achieve an approximate neutrality. In subject, it was probably more at home in print and the classroom than in any of the other media. Over television, it reminded one correspondent of 'a BBC play, done in the original Greek, so nothing would be lost in translation'. It was timed for television, proved too slow for radio, but satisfactory for film and classroom. It was not written in a lineal fashion with an introduction, statement of problem, analysis running from point to point and finally a conclusion, but, like a modern advertisement, took a single idea, stated it immediately, and then sought to achieve multiple perspective by illustrating it in a variety of ways. One student, who recognized this, wrote on her examination: '. . . This was the main point. You made it at the beginning and spent the rest of the time illustrating it.' This non-lineal presentation probably favoured the new media.

Dr. William's article describes the examination, results, and interpretations.

The home television audience was invited to write in, commenting on the show and telling what they understood of the lecture. Some three hundred did so. About a third of the letters were simply requests for copies of the script; the remainder ranged from a few crack-pot replies ('I knew from your face you were just the person who would help me. . . .') to sophisticated, penetrating essays. In fact, the home audience, not the students, wrote by far the best analyses of the lecture.

Announcement of the results (television won, followed by lecture, film, radio, and finally print) evoked considerable interest. Two weeks after the experiment, the senior members of our group appeared as a panel on television and discussed the findings. The CBC then released a publicity statement and the story was picked up by newspapers, including the *New York Times*. All stressed the high score of television and, by implication, its superiority as an educational medium. The president of a local marketing association read the release to a banquet of advertising men with the comment that here, at last, was scientific proof of the superiority of television.

Within a week about 120 letters were received from advertising agencies and groups concerned with educational television. The former were often written in the super-heated jargon of the trade ('Dear Eddie: Your experiment came with providential timing. . . .') and were concerned with one problem: how to sell expensive television time to reluctant advertisers.

Our own reaction was equally revealing. About twenty of us in the seminar placed bets on the outcome. Academics all, we each seriously thought print would win, and merely selected other media as sporting bets. When the results were announced, everyone modified his stand, rationalized the results and said, *naturally* television won.

The reaction within CBC was divided, largely along radio-television lines. This was unfortunate and missed the main point, for the results did not indicate the superiority of one medium over others. They merely directed attention toward differences between them, so great as to be differences of kind rather than degree. Each communication channel codifies reality differently and thus influences, to a surprising degree, the content of the message communicated. It strikes me this approach is more rewarding than the statistical, ho-hum one of most current audience research.

*Edmund S. Carpenter*

### INTRODUCTION

A seminar on culture and communication has frequent cause to concern itself with the mass media. The experiment here reported was the culmination of our first year's effort. While in a very real sense an interdisciplinary product, the responsibility for the design, analysis and presentation of results fell to the psychologists in the seminar as being most familiar with the techniques involved.

Most research on mass media is concerned with either of two objectives: studies of the influence of one medium on attitude changes, and consumer research designed ultimately to help sell soap or whatnot. Little if any work has been done on the degree to which various media facilitate or impede learning, if indeed they have any influence at all. The question does not occur readily because the mass media themselves are seldom seen as educational devices. The silent assumption that mass media exist primarily for entertainment and propaganda, which underlies most such research, automatically excludes research with an educational bias.

### PROBLEM

In its most general form, the problem investigated can be stated thus:

Is learning affected by the channel over which information comes? If so, how and to what extent? While we usually assume that television, for instance, is more compelling than radio in securing our attention, we also assume that we can easily compensate psychologically for this differential advantage. Whenever our attention is really aroused, we can and do attend to the radio address, news or weather report with the firm conviction that we will end up with all the information we require. An extra effort of attention, we assume, will easily make up for the fact that we could have gleaned the same information with less effort over television.

With these considerations in mind, the experiment was designed to provide the 'same' information in the identical wording, to four similar audiences, each of which had the 'same' motivation to seek out and remember the information presented. Given the same objective examination on that information, would the only systematic difference remaining, namely the different media used, make a statistically significant difference to the average scores of those audiences? Television and radio were obvious choices for an experiment on mass communication. Since they are often contrasted with 'real' situations, a 'live' lecture audience was added. The fourth medium chosen was the printed page since it is widely regarded as the essential carrier of Culture—with a capital C—, and is most often thought of as being threatened by the newer media in terms of its continued existence.

DESIGN

From the standpoint of design, all that was required was that the factual content be clearly transmitted without undue distortion over each of the four media and that it be cast in such a way that no one medium was favoured over others. The method employed was the method of constant stimuli whereby the lecturer himself provides the stimulus without reliance on the pecularities of particular medium 'props'. The fact that his gestures, intonations, etc., are differently transmitted by the different media is precisely the point of investigation. That is, since each medium carries the information *in its own way*, do these differences affect the learning process of the audience?

The subjects were 108[1] undergraduates in the General Course in Arts at the University of Toronto, all of whom were studying anthropology as one of five courses comprising their year's work. The lecture topic, 'Thinking Through Language', was unfamiliar to them, and from their point of view, both difficult and stimulating. The class list was arranged

---

[1] Actually the number was larger, but to make the groups as equal as possible and to make the classification on previous academic standing clear, the final number was reduced to 108.

71

in descending order of academic grades, based on first year results, and then arbitrarily divided into four groups or audiences on a stratified sampling basis, such that each audience contained an equal number of high, average and low students. For this purpose, 'high' means grades of A and B+, 'average' means grades of B and B—, 'low' means grades of C+ and below. After the four audiences had been selected in this way, another person arbitrarily assigned each audience to a medium. These were announced to the students on arrival at the CBC studios.

Each group went to a separate room in the CBC buildings where they were supervised by members of the seminar. The lecture was delivered before the studio audience and simultaneously relayed to the television audience and the radio audience. At the same time, mimeographed copies of the lecture were distributed to the reading group, who read at their own speed and for the same length of time as it took to deliver the lecture. Immediately thereafter, each group wrote a thirty minute examination on the lecture. This consisted of nineteen multiple-choice questions (four alternatives each), plus one broad essay type question to be answered in 200–300 words. Most students finished before the nominal time limit. The test should therefore be regarded as a 'power' rather than a 'speed' test. The papers were graded by the anthropology section of the seminar and turned over to the psychology section for analysis.

Here is a section from the lecture and its covering question:

I recall one experience I had several years ago while living with the Eskimos. I was riding along on a dog sled one bitterly cold day—the wind hit me in the back and seemed to come out the other side—when I turned to a hunter with me and said, as best I could in Eskimo, 'The wind is cold.' He roared with laughter. 'How', he asked, 'can the *wind* be cold? *You're* cold, *you're* unhappy. But the *wind* isn't cold or unhappy!' Now this involves more than just another way of speaking; it involves another way of *seeing* things. Consider how different human action must appear when seen through the filter of the Eskimo language where, owing to the lack of transitive or action verbs, it is likely to be perceived as a sort of happening without an active element in it. In Eskimo one cannot say: 'I *kill* him' or 'I *shoot* the arrow', but only 'He dies to me', 'The arrow is flying away from me', just as 'I *hear*' is 'me-sound-is'. Similarly, where we say, 'The lightning *flashed*', as if the lightning *did* something, as if it involved something more than just being lightning, the Eskimo merely says 'Flash'. Eskimo philosophers, if there were any, would be likely to say that what we call action is really a pattern of succeeding impressions.

When we say, 'The lightning flashed' we:
  a  read action into the event
  b  use an intransitive verb
  c  describe the event as being without action
  d  describe the event in the only possible way

The essay question called for an understanding of the whole lecture: 'The lecturer described two native philosophies, but at the same time said that the Eskimos, for example, had no philosophers. How would you interpret these two statements in terms of the lecture?'

CONTROLS

It is a truism that whereas the 19th century public sought to learn the *results* of science, the 20th century public is, more realistically, interested in the *methods* whereby results are achieved. For this reason if for no other, some discussion of the controls used in this study forms an essential part of this report.

The term 'control' itself is a highly ambiguous term, as our seminar quickly learned. As used here, it means only those measures which were taken to hold constant all factors, other than the four media themselves, which might be expected to bias the results.

It does *not* mean that experiments of this type are totalitarian, that social scientists are dictators at heart, that science scorns understanding and seeks only prediction and control, that our subjects were humiliated or 'pushed around' without their consent, that we laboured under the illusion of playing God with other people's lives, that the study was undertaken to fool, bully, delude, hoax or otherwise cajole an innocent group of students.

In terms of controls, the lecturer was his own control. His choice of topic and his organization was his own. The controls were first, that his information be basically accessible via each channel and second, that it should not rely on external 'props' of any kind. Finally, and most difficult of all, the lecture had to be memorized so that the reading group would receive exactly the same content as the other audiences. In order to compensate, as far as possible, for the fact that the reading audience was deprived of both of the sound and sight of the lecturer, certain key words in the mimeographed material were capitalized to give something of the same emphasis they received as delivered.

The subjects were selected to be as homogeneous as possible, i.e., same course, same class and age range, and sharing a common subject matter. Academic ability was controlled by the method of stratified sampling described above, since it was a fair assumption that good students in general learn more than poor ones, even in lectures.

Motivation was controlled by an arrangement with the class instructor who agreed to incorporate performance on our examination into the course term mark. In order to avoid undue anxiety, the arrangement was that those who did well would get a term mark bonus, while those who did indifferently or poorly would suffer no penalty. These factors also operated to produce a good attendance at the studio, and to offset, if not entirely eliminate, factors of personal preference for one or another medium. In addition, the students were fully informed about the experiment and its objectives, and afterwards, were the first group to hear an analysis of the results.

No attempt was made to equate groups for age, sex, socio-economic status, familiarity with television, radio, etc. These were assumed to be roughly controlled (i.e., equated) by random assignment to each group.

The examination was controlled by the use of the objective, multiple-choice type of question, which permits of easy quantification. The score on this section was simply the number right. It should be noted that since each question contained a best answer among the four alternatives presented, the measure yielded is a measure of immediate *recognition*, not recall.

No note-taking was allowed during the lecture, in an attempt to simulate normal conditions of television and radio listening. Whereas the lecturer automatically 'paced' the studio, television and radio audiences, thereby conferring a precise degree of control on them, it was not possible to duplicate this pacing for the reading audience. In this sense, this group was not as well controlled as the others.

RESULTS

The results given here are confined to an analysis of the multiple-choice section of the examination. The statistics used were the analysis of variance and the 't' test of significance[1] of differences between means, i.e., averages.

The analysis of variance showed that media in general *do* make a significant difference in the amount learned as measured by the multiple-choice test. It also showed, as we suspected, that academic ability makes a significant difference in the amount learned. Having established the fact that the four media *per se*, were significant to the learning process, it was then possible to test the audience averages for significance of difference in order to rank them in effectiveness. This analysis showed that the television average was superior to the radio average—significant at the 1% level of confidence (i.e., there are 99 chances in 100 that this is a true difference). It also showed radio to be significantly above both the reading and studio performances—significant at the 5% level of confidence (i.e., there are 95 chances in 100 that this is a true difference).

The graph shows the examination results by audiences and by academic ability, shown here at three levels. This display is more revealing than the averages for each medium, since it shows how the media affect each level of academic ability. The clearest indications come from the television, radio, and reading comparisons, where it can be seen that the media exert their effects at all three academic levels. Note for example that the low students on television do exactly as well as the middle students on radio, a clear instance of medium effect. Note too, that the greatest single discrepancy on the graph occurs between the good students on television and radio. Apparently television has its greatest effect on the best students!

[1] Statistically speaking, a difference between two averages is called significant if it could not have occurred by chance more often than 5 times in 100 occurrences. Therefore, the betting in this study is that we have 95 chances in 100 of being sure that the differences obtained are 'real' differences and not due to chance. In some cases we have 99 chances in 100 of being right.

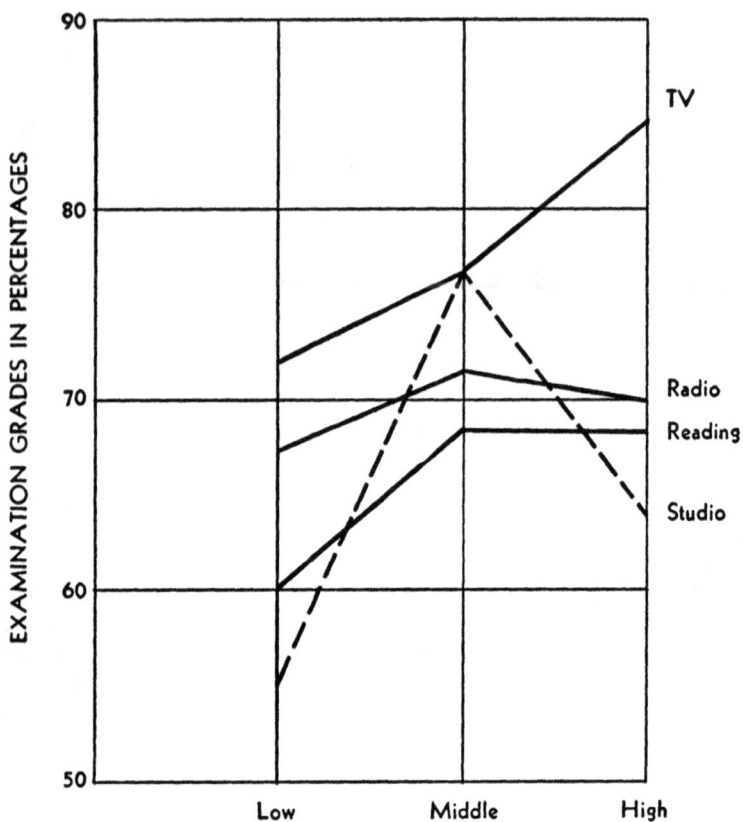

EXAMINATION GRADES IN PERCENTAGES

TV

Radio

Reading

Studio

Low          Middle          High

N = 108 (27 subjects in each audience)
each 'x' represents the average of 9 subjects

## ACADEMIC LEVELS OF STUDENTS

| AUDIENCE | N | MEAN | DIFFERENCE SIGNIFICANT AT |
|---|---|---|---|
| TV | 27 | 77.2% | } 1% level |
| RADIO | 27 | 69.2% | } 5% level |
| READING | 27 | 65.1% | } not sigfct. |
| STUDIO | 27 | 64.9% | |

Table showing average scores by media

The studio results are puzzling. The 'lows' and 'highs' reflect presumably the distractions and excitement of the studio itself, but if they do, why were the middles unaffected by this to the point that they did as well as the television middle group? Originally the studio group was proposed as the equivalent of a lecture audience. One glance at the confusion of the television studio convinced us, *before* the statistical analysis, that whatever this group was, it was *not* a lecture group. We retained it in the study but with the new name 'studio' group.

The table beneath the chart shows the number of cases (N), and the averages for each audience together with the confidence level at which the differences can be accepted as significant.

CONCLUSIONS AND COMMENTS

One experiment does not establish a generalization, but it is plain that under these conditions at least, certain of the mass media, and notably television, are very effective channels for conveying information. The astonishing feature of the study is the relatively poor performance of the reading group. Many members of the seminar predicted it to be the best of the four! One feature involved in these standings became clear from an examination of the results of a single question. In one portion of the talk the lecturer stressed gestures and delivery to accent his words; the question covering this passage was accurately answered by most of the television audience, half the radio audience and few of the reading audience.

It is then fair to conclude that media do make a difference in immediate recognition, using undergraduates as subjects. It is also fair to rank the media from television through radio to reading in terms of their effectiveness *under these conditions*. No conclusion is drawn on the studio group.

At this stage of research, generalization is dangerous. The study does not prove that television is 'better' than radio or that either is preferable to books, or that 'live' audiences learn little. Would one get similar results with housewives, with engineers or even with these same students presented with a totally unfamiliar topic, say, the devolution of estates in Athenian law? Would persons of average or below average intelligence react in the same way? Would children? These and a host of similar questions suggest that at least an interesting and important area of research has been tapped by this exploration.

*D. C. Williams*

Ethnography, like all other branches of science in the USSR, gets the fullest support and attention of the Soviet Government.

During the very first years of Soviet power, a number of measures were carried out aimed at promoting the all-round development of ethnographic research in the country: several ethnographic institutions were set up; departments of ethnography were opened at universities; and numerous expeditions were fitted out to various parts of the country. Local residents who knew their native parts well began to be drawn into the scientific work in ethnography on a broad scale. And this became the first important feature specific to the work of Soviet ethnographers.

During the period of formation of the multi-national Soviet state a second characteristic feature of Soviet ethnography became defined—its connection with the problems of Socialist transformation of the culture and life of the peoples of the USSR. To determine the state boundaries of Central Asian republics in conformity with the national composition of the population, to set up national areas in the Far North inhabited by a great many ethnic groups, and to carry out other such important measures of Soviet power, it was necessary to make a profound study of the ethnic composition of the population and the specific national features of their culture.

From year to year the work in ethnography grew in scale, theoretical research became more profound, and new personnel swelled the ranks of the country's ethnographers, in particular, from among the various nationalities which only under the Soviet system had given rise to their own national intelligentsia.

*The Centres of Ethnographic Research in the USSR*

The main scientific centre of ethnographic research in the USSR is the Miklukho-Maklai Institute of Ethnography of the USSR Academy of Sciences. The director of this Institute is corresponding member of the Academy of Sciences of the USSR S. P. Tolstov. The Institute is comprised of a number of sections: the Slavic-Russian, the non-Slavic peoples of Europe, the Near and the Middle East, the Caucasus, Siberia, East and South Asia, Africa, America, Australia and Oceania. Besides, there are sections devoted to ethnic statistics and cartography, and anthropology, and a plastic anthropological reconstruction laboratory headed by M. M. Gerasimov, whose work in restoring the facial features of man from the skull is no doubt the most successful of its kind in world anthropology (a monograph by Gerasimov called *Restoration of the Facial Features from the Skull,* which was published back in 1949, is now coming out in a second, considerably enlarged edition).

Functioning in Leningrad is a Branch of the Institute of Ethnography and the Peter the Great Museum of Anthropology and Ethnography, which is the country's biggest repository of ethnographical, anthropological and primeval archeological collections. In postwar years the museum has resumed publication of the special collections of materials on anthropology and ethnography that it had been putting out ever since 1901. In Leningrad too there is a State Museum of Ethnography of the Peoples of the USSR.

Functioning within the framework of the Miklukho-Maklai Institute is the comprehensive Khoresm archeological and ethnographical expedition, whose discoveries are known to world science. The results of the expedition's work are dealt with in a number of publications, notable among which are the monograph by S. P. Tolstov *Ancient Khorezm* that merited a Stalin Prize First Class and the first volume of works of the expedition that came out in 1952.

There are ethnographic institutions in all sixteen of the constituent Soviet republics (within the framework of the Academies of Sciences in the republics or the Branches of the Academy of Sciences of the USSR) and in most of the autonomous republics and regions. A number of the republics and regions have museums of ethnography containing valuable exhibits.

The central printed organ of Soviet ethnographers is the journal *Soviet Ethnography*, published by the Academy of Sciences of the USSR. The Miklukho-Maklai Institute regularly publishes scientific researches in ethnography and anthropology. Among the publications of recent years mention should be made of the following: *Ancient Khorezm* by S. P. Tolstov, *Restoration of the Facial Features from the Skull*, by M. M. Gerasimov, *Ethnic Boundaries and Ethnic Territories* by P. I. Kushner, *Tribal Society* under the editorship of S. P. Tolstov, and *The Origin of Man and the Ancient Distribution of the Human Race* under the editorship of M. G. Levin. Current research of the institute is dealt with in special issues of *Brief Communications of the Institute of Ethnography of the Academy of Sciences of the USSR*.

The results of the work of other ethnographic institutions are presented in the numerous publications of the Academies of Sciences in the republics, of the universities, and other establishments. Thus, the work of a group of Georgian ethnographers headed by G. S. Chitai, for example, has been published by the Academy of Sciences of the Georgian Soviet Socialist Republic, and the work of Professor N. I. Vorobyov on the ethnography of the Tatars has been put out by the Kazan Branch of the Academy of Sciences of the USSR. Research work in ethnography is published in Yakutsk, Abakan (center of the Khakass Autonomous Region), Nukus (capital of the Kara-Kalpak Autonomous Republic), Syktyvkar (center of the Komi Autonomous Republic) and in other centers of once backward outlying districts of the country.

*The Main Problems on Which Soviet Ethnographers are now Working*

As distinct from the history of culture, functional and psychological schools that are the most widespread in the capitalist countries, the Soviet school of ethnography proceeds from recognition of the decisive role of material production in the history of society and the identity of paths that all the peoples of the world have traversed and are now traversing in their development. In studying one or another element of material culture, one or another phenomenon in social and spiritual life, Soviet ethnographers discern in them first and foremost a reflection of a definite stage of development of society. This in no way excludes but on the contrary presupposes a profound study of the concrete history of the

80

given phenomenon, of the way it spread and changed in form among different peoples. Not denying the role of the influence of the culture of one people upon the culture of another pople, Soviet ethnographers cannot however attach to this factor the inordinate importance that the supporters of the diffusion trend in ethnography attach to it. Alien to Soviet ethnographic science are the principles of the psychological school, a school that builds up 'cultural models' for the different peoples, denies common lines of development of the human race and revives in this way the ideas of racism, ideas most inimical to the spirit of progress and humanism.

In the USSR research in the field of ethnography is closely bound up with the most urgent tasks in the development of Soviet society. In their latest researches Soviet ethnographers devote a great deal of attention to a study of the new forms of culture and conditions of life which are being created among the various peoples of the Soviet land in connection with the Socialist forms of economy. At present a number of monographs devoted to this subject are being prepared for publication.

A big series of researches is connected with the study of the origin, ethnic history and the history of the culture of the various peoples inhabiting the Soviet Union. These researches have now acquired special significance in connection with the work of Soviet historians in preparing courses of the history of the peoples who until the October Revolution did not have their own written history, and in some cases their own written language as well. In this series of researches mention should be made among others of *Essays on the History of the Altai People* by Professor L. P. Potapov, which merited a Stalin Prize; the researches of B. O. Dolgikh, who for the first time restored on the basis of extensive data the picture of the settlement of the tribes and peoples of Siberia in the 17th century, and the *Essays on the Historic Ethnography of the Karakalpakians* by T. A. Zhdanko.

Study of the history and modern culture of the peoples involves the collection of field data. From year to year the Institute of Ethnography of the Academy of Sciences of the USSR and other scientific institutions of the country fit out expeditions to various parts of the Soviet Union. Thus in 1953, for example, the Institute of Ethnography alone organized the following expeditions: the Khoresm, Kirghiz, Daghestan, Sayano-Altai (the Tuva Autonomous Region), the Russian (which worked in the districts of Central Russia), the Baltic (which worked on the territory of the Latvian, Lithuanian and Estonian Soviet Socialist Republics) and the Moldavian. Of the expeditions of past years mention should be made of the North-Eastern, which worked over a period of several years on Chukotka, Kamchatka and the Amur, and also the Taimyr and the Tajik expeditions.

Concentrating their main attention on the study of the ethnography of the peoples of the USSR, Soviet scientists are at the same time devoting part of their research to study of the ethnography of the peoples of countries abroad, and in particular of the peoples of the colonial and dependent countries. The researches in the field of the history and modern culture of these peoples carried out by Soviet ethnographers fully reveal the complete groundlessness of the view widespread in capitalist countries that the colonial peoples are incapable of independent development. Facts show that the cause of the present backwardness of these peoples lies by no means in their innate mental abilities like certain bourgeois scientists claim but mainly in the conditions which have been created for them by the colonial powers.

For a number of years now the Miklukho-Maklai Institute of Ethnography has been preparing for publication a work in many volumes called *The Peoples of the World* (under the general editorship of corresponding member of the Academy of Sciences of the USSR S. P. Tolstov), which will give an ethnographic characteristic of the peoples of all parts of the world. Due to come off the press shortly are the volumes: *The Peoples of Africa* under the editorship of Professors D. A. Olderogge and I. I. Potekhin, *The Peoples of Australia and Oceania* under the editorship of S. A. Tokarev, and *The Peoples of Siberia* under the editorship of Professors L. P. Potapov and M. G. Levin. In collaboration with the Department of Ethnography of Moscow University, a textbook on general ethnography has been prepared under the editorship of Professor N. N. Cheboksarov.

Parallel with work on the aforementioned problems, Soviet ethnographers are directing their efforts to a further study of the history of primitive society. Much attention is being paid to research on the problem of matriarchy. A book by Professor M. O. Kosven called *Matriarchy* is devoted to this problem. Soviet scientists are also continuing to give thought to such problems as the origin of exogamy, the beginning of dual organization, and the historical relation of the clan and the tribe.

Soviet ethnographers highly value the heritage left them by progressive ethnographers of the past, among whom they pronounce the name of Lewis Morgan with especial respect.

Many urgent problems of ethnography require exchange of opinion of the ethnographers of different countries. Soviet ethnographers, like all Soviet scientists, are ardent supporters of consolidation in every possible way of scientific ties with their colleagues abroad.

*I. Potekhin and M. Levin*

## CONCEPT OF MONOPOLY AND CIVILIZATION

INTRODUCTORY NOTE

In his writings on the communication networks of empires past and present, Dr. Harold A. Innis sought to develop, as he put it, 'general concepts at the basis of progress and the adjustment of order to meet the demands of change'. In the essay which follows the space-time problems of political organisation are examined in the light of concepts he had found useful in his historical studies of changing media of communication. His untimely death in 1952 cut short his explorations, but he left behind him a very considerable amount of work in process including a massive history of communication and a number of shorter pieces of which this is one. No attempt has been made to revise it as he would have done, but although it is not in the form in which he would have presented it for publication, in its tone and method and the questions it raises the essay provides a useful introduction to his later writings on communication. Exploratory in spirit, tentative in its conclusions, it reflects nevertheless his intense dislike of monopolies of knowledge which appeared to him to be productive of bias in communication fatal to mutual understanding among peoples and nations. Changes in communication media provide the key to analysis of problems of competition and monopoly, change and order, growth and decay, problems seldom more pressing than in the chaotic mid-20th century in which he lived. He wrote as a historian concerned with contempory developments and his work must be evaluated in this light.[1]

A complete bibliography of Dr. Innis' writings (ed. Jane Ward) appears in the *Canadian Journal of Economics and Political Science,* May, 1953. His published works on communication include *Empire and Communication,* Clarendon Press, 1950; *The Bias of Communication,* University of Toronto Press, 1951; and *Changing Concepts of Time,* University of Toronto Press, 1952. At present there is in preparation his history of communication (eds. Mary and Donald Innis), a collection of his major essays, and a memorial volume (ed. S. D. Clark).

*W. T. Easterbrook*

THE CONCEPT OF MONOPOLY AND CIVILIZATION

I am taking advantage of this opportunity to put before you questions which have worried me in research on the character of civilizations and to solicit your advice. I have been concerned with the possible extension of concepts in the special field of economics and in particular the concept of monopoly notably in knowledge. Since the first World War the study of civilization has been threatened by two monopolies, the first in Germany represented by Spengler, and the second in Great Britain or possibly the English-speaking world represented by Toynbee.

In the United States, Sorokin, a Russian exile, and Kroeber, of German descent, have developed elaborate approaches. In France you have been critical—I refer particularly to Prof. Lucien Febvre—of such monopolies. As has been the case in the past we look to you for criticism of inclusive systems.

I am under special obligation to such criticism and to special studies in attempting to develop an approach to the study of civilizations through the subject of communications and of monopolies in relation to them. I shall not refer to special studies such as those in the history of civilization series but my remarks will indicate my debt to them. In confining my comments to political organizations, I shall restrict my attention to two dimensions—on the one hand the length of time over which the organiza-

---

[1] For recent appraisals of his work, the following should be consulted: V. W. Bladen and others, *American Economic Review,* May, 1953; A. Brady, *Canadian Journal of Economics and Political Science,* February, 1953; J. B. Brebner, *Economic Journal,* September, 1953; A. H. Cole, *Economic History Review,* December, 1953; D. G. Creighton, *Canadian Historical Review,* December, 1952; W. T. Easterbrook, *Canadian Journal of Economics and Political Science,* August, 1953; A. Faucher, *La Revue de l'University Laval,* September, 1953; W. A. Mackintosh, *Journal of Political Economy,* June, 1953; H. M. McLuhan, *Queen's Quarterly,* Autumn, 1953.

tion persists and on the other hand the territorial space brought within its control. It will be obvious in the case of the second consideration that organization will be dependent to an important extent on communications in a broad sense—roads, vehicles of transmission, especially horses, postal organization and the like for carrying out orders. It will be less obvious that effective communication will be dependent on the diffusion of a knowledge of writing or in turn a knowledge of an alphabet through which orders may be disseminated among a large number of subjects.

A discussion of the other dimensions of a political organization, namely duration, raises numerous problems. Examples of organizations which have persisted over a long period such as the Roman, late Roman and Byzantine empires suggest that attention must have been given not only to the administration of territorial space but also to ways and means by which survival was achieved. Obvious devices involved with the problem of duration were the organization of force notably in defence and the encouragement of industry and trade essential for the support of defence. Force in itself implies a hierarchical arrangement but also an arrangement which permits rapid advancement of ability to the top. Every soldier must carry a marshal's baton in his knapsack.

The problem of force arises from its inability to emphasize its limitations and from its tendency to make increasingly heavy demands on the resources of the country it is concerned in protecting. The Byzantine army seems to have been built up with a view to using the smallest possible resources with the greatest possible effectiveness. Changes in dynasties suggest that it was not too difficult for able soldiers like Justin and others to reach the position of emperor. It assumes that the necessity of employment of force is sufficiently continuous to maintain an effective demand for ability at higher levels in the army and that a military bureaucracy does not become stale. The dangers of a dynasty in which able leadership tends to die out with successive generations, are avoided by the pitiless demands of force.

The limitations of force in maintaining continuity may be offset by reliance on religion. Belief resting on ritual with an emphasis on the oral tradition and on hierarchical organizaton, is adapted primarily to a concern with duration and with control over time. Death itself as an obvious permanent phenomenon was used as a concept emphasizing continuity particularly in relation to immortality.

Religion linked to force, as in the Byzantine empire following Constantine's recognition of Christianity, made it possible to enlist the

86

support of culture and in particular, the arts. In architecture a capital city designed to reinforce the prestige of force may be supplemented by ecclesiastical buildings as in the case of St. Sophia. Imperial ceremony may be joined to religious ritual. Sculpture will reflect the demands of religion and of the state—so too, will painting. It has been said that religion is a good servant but a bad master; there is evidence that it may not even be the best servant. The conservative and rigid character of belief restricts its adaptability to the demands of force and an effective hierarchy, which enlists the ablest minds and places them at its head, may insist on a position which will embarass, if not threaten the state, as in the case of the iconoclastic controversy.

I have ventured these remarks by way of illustrating the problem of a political organization in relation to territorial space and duration in time. I shall now attempt to discuss the problem of a political organization in relation to monopolies which develop in relation to space and in relation to time. It appears that the problem of spatial organization was more or less effectively worked out in Babylon, and the problem of time organization in Egypt. In Mesopotamia, religious organization, centering in the City state, was concerned with the development of knowledge, particularly in language and mathematics essential to economic organization and determined to an important extent by the character of its medium, namely clay. Sumerian culture provided a nucleus of organized knowledge and an emphasis on continuity in religious organization which supported the development of political organizations in the empire of Sargon, in the restoration of dynasties centering on Ur, in the empire of Hammurbi and of its successor under the Kassites. In turn the Hittite, the Assyrian and the Persian empires paid Sumerian culture the tribute of recognition or of imitation. While the monopoly of knowledge and the control over time reflected in the persistence of Sumerian culture contributed to the effectiveness of political organization, it was in turn a source of weakness to successive empires and contributed to their disappearance.

In Egypt religious organizations emerged in relation to the king or to political organization possibly on the occasion of the joining of two kingdoms, the north and the south. The power of the combination was evident in the pyramids of stone and in the development of the concept of immortality. Death became a support to continuity. The burden of the demands became evident in a decline in the absolute position of the king, in the emergence of a religious organization and in the development of an oligarchy in which immortality was extended to the people. Decline of political organization was evident in the success of the invasion of the Hyksos. But the tenacity of religion supported a re-organization of force, expulsion of the Hyksos and the extension of control over space in the Egyptian empire. Again its demands were responsible for a succession of dynasties and for their collapse in the face of extension of the Assyrian, the Persian and the Alexandrian empires. The monopoly of knowledge controlled by religion was determined to an important extent by the character of writing, namely hieroglyphics and its medium, namely papyrus and the brush.

The limitations of monopolies of knowledge in Babylonia and in Egypt shown in the instability of political organizations were evident in the emergence of simpler forms of writing centering around the alphabet which developed among peoples who were marginal to the influence of the two regions. The alphabet responded to the demands of a spoken language by linking sound to letter. The Greeks carried the adaptability of the alphabet to the point of developing certain letters as vowels. An escape from the limitations of the monopolies of knowledge of Egypt and Mesopotamia and the adaptation of the alphabet to the demands of a powerful oral tradition were evident in the freshness and flexibility of Greek culture in the fifth century and its emergence as the basis of Western civilization as contrasted with civilizations of the Far East and of the Americas.

The adaptability of the alphabet to the spoken language created new problems of monopoly in that spoken languages which differed materially were crystallized in a written language and great effort was necessary to develop understanding over a vast area and with different languages. In the Alexandrian empire and the Hellenistic kingdoms the limitations of language were evident in the necessity of relying on a religion based on the deification of kings, in problems of continuity of political organizations, and in their absorption by the Roman empire. With the extension of control over territorial space including diversity of languages and dependence on organized force in the Roman empire, religion proved an inadequate support. The choice of Constantinople for defensive purposes as a capital of the Empire was accompanied by an acceptance of Christianity which would enlist the co-operation of eastern Hellenistic populations. As we have suggested, a balance of control over monopolies of time and monopolies of space explained the success evident in the duration of the Byzantine empire.

In the West decline of control over territorial space in the face of barbarian invasions led to an emphasis on control over time and religion. In the words of Gibbon it was characterized by the rise of barbarism and religion. In this monopoly, emphasis was placed on Latin as a language and as a device to offset the divisive influence of several languages. A monopoly was built up through dependence on a limited body of scriptural writings on a relatively permanent medium namely parchment. A hierarchical organization was strengthened by development of ritual, a concern with monasticism and celibacy, and the emergence of Gothic architecture. The effects of the monopoly were evident in the position of the papacy and its control over knowledge and in the inquisition.

A monopoly over time invited competition such as that which followed a spread in the use of paper from China through the Mohammedans at Bagdad and Cordova and in the recognition of new sources of learning, notably in Greek science and philosophy represented especially by Aristotle filtered through Arabic or coming direct from Constantinople. In the competitive strife the monopoly of Latin as a language was destroyed and increasing supplies of cheap paper supported the growth of a literature of the vernacular as in Italy and France and the Reformation as in Germany, the Netherlands and England. It would be instructive to trace the influence of paper on the development of writing and of printing, particularly in Germany on which the Roman empire had made little impression and which was marginal to France in which copyists exercised an important monopoly and in Italy which had witnessed an expansion of the paper industry. In any case the vernaculars emerged in different regions and became an ultimate determinant of political boundaries.

The modern state with political boundaries influenced by the paper and printing industries has been profoundly affected by the industrial revolution and the application of steam power to the paper and printing industries especially in the latter part of the 19th. century. The divisive influence of these industries has been evident in the divisions of regions speaking the same language as in the separation of the United States from the British Empire, in the emergence of the British Commonwealth of Nations and in the growth of regionalism centering around large metropolitan areas. Freedom of the press has been given constitutional guarantees as in the United States or guarantees in other forms as in other countries and has provided bulwarks for monopolies which have emphasized control over space. Under these circumstances the problem of duration or monopoly over time has been neglected, indeed obliterated. Time has been cut into pieces the length of a day's newspaper. The tyranny of monopoly over space in its emphasis on change and instability has assumed graver threats to continuity than the tyranny of monopoly over time in the Middle Ages to the establishment of political organization. It may be that the concept of progress arises from the effects of a swing from a type of monopoly concerned with control over time to a type of monopoly concerned with control over space and that we favour this type of change in contrast with a civilization which assumes control over space and time which seems to us to favour stability and possibly stagnation.

*H. A. Innis*

INTRODUCTION

'The polished essay was introduced as a clever contrivance adopted by a former dynasty to prevent the literate from thinking too much!' The reader of the later Innis will never encounter any of these clever contrivances for lotos eaters. Not exemption from but unremitting appeal to thought is characteristic of his later work. If one were asked to state briefly the basic change which occurred in the thought of Innis in his last decade, it could be said that he shifted his attention from the trade-routes of the external world to the trade-routes of the mind. Technology, he saw, had solved the problem of production of commodities and had already turned to the packaging of information. And the penetrative powers of the pricing system were as nothing beside the power of the new media of communication to penetrate and transform all existing institutions and patterns of thought.

The comments which follow were taken from a number of graduate essays from a seminar on culture and communication at the University of Toronto this last year.

*Marshall McLuhan*

Innis saw Western history as beginning with temporal organization and ending with spatial organization. Between these lay a series of major technological innovations, each giving rise to a new medium of communication. Each medium in turn eventually resulted in a monopoly of knowledge which destroyed the conditions suited to creative thought and was displaced by a medium with its peculiar type of monopoly of knowledge. And each, over a long period, determined to some extent the character of knowledge communicated. There were, of course, countless other innovations, but for Innis, history, from the beginnings of writing to the invention of the printing press, was divided into four major eras, dominated successively by the use of clay, papyrus, parchment and paper as communication media. Each era he sub-divided according to the type of script employed and type of writing implement used.

Although Innis failed to define, precisely, what he meant by 'oral tradition', his frequent references to Homer leave little doubt as to his position. He meant essentially what the words imply—a selection, from the history of a people, of a series of related events, culturally defined as significant, and their oral transmission from generation to generation. Ultimately, of course, the oral tradition of the Greeks was committed to writing; but it remained an oral tradition. Growing out of innumerable face-to-face contacts, endlessly modified in accordance with changing circumstances, the poems of Homer were 'the work of generations of reciters and minstrels and reflected the demands of generations of audiences to whom they were recited'. They were a link with the living past of all concerned. Their recitation was a social occasion, symbolic both of continuity in time and social cohesion in the present. The minstrel was immediately aware of the effect of his performance on the audience, and the audience immediately and directly responded. The content, then, was a series of past events that not only helped to share the present, but gave it meaning and significance. The oral tradition was a total process in the sense that the entire group was involved; the most significant and enduring product of this process was the cohesion and continuity of the group itself.

Perhaps the most significant characteristic of an oral tradition was its flexibility and persistence. Because it was rooted in the feelings, attitudes, and linguistic habits of the people, it was difficult to destroy. Through the process of endless repetition it 'created recognized standards and lasting moral and social institutions; it built up the soul of social organizations and maintained their continuity; and it developed ways of perpetuating itself. The oral tradition and religion served almost the same purpose.'

The fact that Greece was marginal to the older civilizations of Egypt and the Near East enabled her to develop the oral tradition in relative isolation. At this point in history, writing was common to the Near East, Egypt and Greece, with a generic relationship between the various alphabets in use. Yet there was a significant difference. In Greece, writing was subordinated to the demands of an oral tradition; among her neighbours, it was an esoteric craft used by secular and religious rules to maintain a monopoly of knowledge and their own social dominance.

Western civilization, in Innis' terms, is a composite structure embracing the oral traditions of the Greeks and Hebrews and the written traditions of Egypt and the Near East. The first was concerned with temporal orientation, that is, with continuity, and became tangible when 'religious monopolies concerned with time relied on the oral tradition'. The second, concerned with spatial orientation, was based on written laws and the army, and was ancestral to the modern state.

To the traditional historical sequence—Rome, Holy Roman Empire, Rise of Nationalism—Innis equated the communication sequence—papyrus, parchment, printing—although the correspondence was not absolute, of course. As the alliance of church and state persisted, each became increasingly dependent on various systems of writing. Each system, in turn, resulted in increasing rigidity that was expressed in a monopoly of knowledge. But the oral tradition persisted with varying intensity, and on the periphery of the area in which the monopoly of knowledge was operative, it was relatively unimpaired. It was probably not fortuitous that 'the printing industry made rapid advances in regions in which the effects of the Roman conquest were limited such as Germany and England or in regions marginal to areas dominated by a bureaucracy based on papyrus'.

The dilemma of our age is that each new medium of communication actually reduces communication. 'Technological advance in communication implies a narrowing of the range from which material is distributed and a widening of the range of reception, so that large numbers receive, but are unable to make any direct response. Those on the receiving end of material from a mechanized central system are precluded from participation in healthy, vigorous, and vital discussion.' In its broadest sense, communication is the sum-total of those relationships that unite an individual with the world and the people around him. The dependence on mass media reduces the complex network of human relationships to a mechanical reiteration of statements that become increasingly meaningless.

Innis was concerned that the traditions of the university, centering around the direct oral method of instruction, had been weakened by the impact of mechanization. Emphasis on books led to increasing sterility; the harassed teacher discovered that 'ideas must be ground down to a convenient size to meet the demands of large numbers'; the art of teaching was reduced to pedagogical industry. 'Large ideas can only be conceived after intensive study over a long period and through the direct and powerful device of the spoken word in small groups.'

To Innis, social stability depended upon a proper balance between the written and oral traditions. The written tradition relates to the State, provides spatial stability and is necessary for the dissemination of facts; the oral tradition, rooted in the feelings, linguistic habits and attitudes of the people, alone can maintain a sense of social continuity.

*Walter Kenyon*

### INNIS AND ANTHROPOLOGY

Innis' literary career may be divided into several periods, each marked by ever-expanding social interests. In the last of these he became interested in anthropology and related subjects, and turned to the study of culture.

As a historian in the role of anthropologist, he employed, in the widest meaning of these terms, a historical-functional model. Historical as evidenced by a diachronic interest in cultural development and change; functional insofar as he was concerned with the consequences which a given communication medium had for both the maintenance of equilibrium and the eventual survival of a society.

*The Bias of Communication* was intended as a footnote to Kroeber's *Configurations of Culture Growth*, but it proved to be much more than this. Where Kroeber avoided causes, limiting his study to a description of cultural growth and decline, Innis saw in these configurations the operation of an invariant. While Kroeber discovered no 'laws' in culture history, 'nothing cyclical, regularly repetitive, or necessary', Innis perceived a causal factor which, though not 'natural' or 'teleological', could nevertheless account for both cultural stability and change. This invariant he called the bias or imbalance which developed in the dimensions of the communication channel. Specifically, he held that the knowledge a people possessed, as expressed in their time-space concepts, related to the physical nature of their communication media.

Anthropological and historical literature revealed to him the operation of two distinct, often mutually exclusive communication means—the oral and the written. The former, he found, was predominantly rooted in time, the latter in space. Ideally both needed to be considered by any society that expected to survive and prosper, but history reveals that this was rarely the case. As culture grew and 'sacred' became 'secular' the oral gave way to the written. Time considerations were replaced by the needs of space. Growth and technology put a premium upon those media which fostered administrative efficiency. It was this bias, this over-emphasis of one tradition in favour of the other, that was the dynamic which, to Innis, accounted for the rise and fall of culture.

Culture is concerned with the capacity of the individual to appraise problems in terms of space and time and with enabling him to take the proper steps at the right time. It is at this point that the tragedy of modern culture has arisen as inventions in commercialism have destroyed a sense of time.

Throughout his work Innis reiterated the close connection between culture and time, and warned against its neglect. He saw the present trend, with its over-emphasis upon space as a result of the preponderance of media designed to ensure the success of bureaucratic governments, as the beginning of the collapse of Western civilization. A balance between these two traditions—one oral, temporal and democratic, the other written, spatial and autocratic—was to Innis not only the dynamic model, but the ideal society. Balance between these poles held the potentiality for dynamic process: the functioning, enduring society. Imbalance brought disruption and change.

Though polarized for comparison, these traditions were theoretically ideal types. Time and things spatial were related to one; space and things spatial to the other. These were not formal definitions, but specifications of characteristics. Thus, 'An oral tradition implies freshness and elasticity, but students of anthropology have pointed to the binding character of custom in primitive culture.' The 'freshness and elasticity' are specifications of the ideal type; they stem from the nature of the medium, not from the context of custom. They are not space-bound. The oral could be written, and yet retain its freshness and elasticity: it was by Plato and the early Greeks by the use of dialogue. Presented spatially, it still remained temporally oriented. It is from this point of view that Innis' trenchant remark becomes clear: 'The ancient world troubled about sounds, the modern world about thoughts.'

Innis' brief acquaintance with anthropology had a number of effects upon his perspective, not the least of which was a shift toward humanism. Not only did he become concerned with the social implications of economics but also with man's role in culture as creator and created. This is particularly evident where culture becomes the measure of all things, and the means to attain the good life. As a facet of the oral tradition, he found the attainment of these ideals blocked where time considerations were set aside in favour of space.

There are parallels here between his work and that of much contemporary anthropology. Redfield, for example, suggests a dual system, quite similar to Innis', for comparing human social behaviour. In contrasting the order whereby activities of men in preliterate as against urban societies are coordinated, he finds the former characterized by a moral order, the latter by a technical one. The moral order emphasizes human sentiments and the good life. It has depth and is steeped in tradition. It is supported by supernatural sanction. The technical order is not so founded. It can exist without the knowledge of those bound together that they are so bound. It is anonymous. It is structured spatially. It evaluates by performance, not by social ascription. 'In the technical order men are bound by things, or are themselves things. They are organized by necessity and expediency.'

Innis demonstrates the dangers involved in neglecting time and the oral tradition, but he overlooks difficulties inherent in this view. His insistence upon a return to tradition as the way to save the Western world is practically a mandate to embrace organized religion. But there is little evidence that this will save society, any more than it saved the Roman world after its conversion to Christianity.

*Robert C. Dailey*

INNIS' METHOD

To present a dynamic model in print is difficult. A multiplicity of simultaneous events occurring in different places cannot easily be communicated within the limits imposed by the temporal sequence of words and sentences. Innis solved the problem by avoiding lineality and presenting rapid shots of events separated widely in space and time. His presentation gives the impression of multiple relationships between parts of a mosaic; it forces attention on the dynamism inherent in the model. Consider the following paragraph:

Regularity of work brought administration, increase in production, trade, and the growth of cities. The spread of mathematics from India to Baghdad and the Moorish universities of Spain implied the gradual substitution of Arabic for Roman numerals and an enormous increase in the efficiency of calculation. Measurement of time facilitated the use of credit, the rise of exchanges, and calculations of the predictable future essential to the development of insurance. Introduction of paper, and invention of the printing press hastened the decline of Latin and the rise of vernaculars. Science met the demands of navigation, industry, trade, and finance by the development of astronomy and refined measurements of time which left little place for myth or religion. The printing press supported the Reformation and destroyed the monopoly of the church over time though the persistence of its interest is evident in feast days. The church recognized at an early date the threat of astronomers to the monopoly over time and treated them accordingly.

The impression created by this disconnected style is enhanced by enormous condensation. Gilzean-Reid and MacDonald wrote:

'. . . between the years 1868 and 1874 a great change came over journalism, and more especially to London journalism. News from all parts of the world naturally gravitated to London. From London to the provinces the only mode of transmission was the railway, and consequently the provinces bought the London papers instead of establishing their own; but the invention of the telegraph deprived London of that monopoly which the railway had conferred upon it. . . . Reform Bill of 1868 did more than enlarge the number of those having political power; it made them think; it created 'provincial opinion'; the London monopoly was broken through.

In Innis, this paragraph becomes: 'The monopoly of London strengthened by the railway, was destroyed by the invention of the telegraph which encouraged provincial competition after 1868.'

Such compression makes each page a wealth of information, but it also makes each page a problem in comprehension, further complicated by the fact that statements are taken out of context and juxtaposed with sentences referring to different periods.

In his work on the history of civilizations, Innis relied on secondary sources. An omnivorous reader, he covered many disciplines and all his writings are filled with references from various fields. Research, to him, became a problem of locating and selecting material to amplify his thesis, which he had previously worked out in the field of Canadian history and was now applying to civilization generally.

He included and emphasized only those data which supported his argument. All history fell neatly into the framework he postulated. Fragments of data fitted together to make up smoothly functioning models of empires, civilizations, industries and media of communication.

On the floor in Innis' office there were literally piles of references and quotations—each pile a book in the making. He wrote too much and quoted too frequently to waste time with copyrights. When he wanted to quote something, he either just used a line or two, or paraphased, and then went on with his writing.

*Endel Tulving*

INNIS AND TIME

Innis' communication studies were intended to supply a sense of balance to the modern mind confronted with mass communication problems. The contemporary bias for space needed to be balanced with the demands of time. 'We must somehow escape on the one hand from our obsession with the moment and on the other hand from our obsession with history. In freeing ourselves from time and attempting a balance between the demands of time and space we can develop conditions favorable to an interest in cultural activity.' His analysis of media biases for time or for space, for endurance or extension, convinced him of the need for their synthesis in any stable communication system.

To thoroughly grasp his attitude towards time, it is necessary to turn to the war against the time cult that was waged by Wyndham Lewis in the 1920's and which has become even more relevant today. *Time and Western Man* and *The Art of Being Ruled* stand as key analyses of the inter-penetration of time philosophy at all levels of life, from the popular music hall and business world to the arts, sciences and philosophy.

Wyndham Lewis has argued that the fashionable mind is the time-denying mind. The results of development in communication are reflected in the time philosophy of Bergson, Einstein, Whitehead, Alexander and Russell. In Bergson we have glorification of the moment with no reference beyond itself and no absolute or universal value.

'The world in which advertisement dwells is a one-day world', Innis cites from Lewis. This is the Bergsonian world of time as sensation, the business world where 'Time is money', the advertising world which is 'necessarily a plane universe without depth. Upon this Time lays down discontinuous entities, side by side; each day, each temporal entity, complete in itself with no perspective, no fundamental exterior reference at all.'

The advertising world carries the mechanization of the word a step higher by mechanizing the image. An emphasis on time is reflected by the 'dateline' of the popular press. These phenomena are reinforced by toilet-training, feeding schedules, train schedules (the commuting world makes Mr. 6:10 a reality) and the well-run suburban household—all integrated towards the mechanical movement of personality. The rhythm of life is distorted into the dance of death:

I prefer the prose-movement—easy, uncontrolled and large—to the insistent, hypnotic rhythm favoured by the most fashionable political thought in the West. For me, there should be no adventitiously imposed *rhythm* for life in the rough. Life in the rough, or on the average, should be there in its natural grace, chaos, and beauty; not cut down and arranged into a machine-made system. Its natural gait and movement it derives from cosmic existence; and where too obsessing a human law— or time, or beat—gets imposed upon it, the life and beauty depart from it. *Musical-politics,* as the uplift politics of millenial doctrine can be termed—are, without any disguise, the politics of hypnotism, enregimentation, the sleep of the dance.

*Donald Theall*

'Tis we, who, lost in stormy visions, keep
With phantoms an unprofitable strife,
And in mad trance strike with our spirit's knife
Invulnerable nothings—

*Adonais*, xxxix

There are three accounts of the incident at Tanyrallt which derive from persons who were directly concerned in the affair and its immediate aftermath. The first in origin, though not in being written down, records Shelley's version of the event given within a few hours after it occurred:

... Mr. Williams was sent for, and found Mr. Shelley in a sad state of distress and excitement; he had fancied that he saw a man's face on the drawing-room window; he took his pistol and shot the glass to shivers, and then bounced out on the grass, and there he saw leaning against a tree the ghost, or, as he said, the devil; and to show Mr. Williams what he had seen, he took his pen and ink and sketched the figure on the screen, where it *is* at this moment, showing plainly that his mind was astray. . . . When I add that Mr. Shelley set fire to the wood to burn the apparition (with some trouble they were saved), you may suppose it was not all right with him. . . .[1]

The second account consists of Shelley's own brief references to the affair in letters written within a few days of it:

I have just escaped an atrocious assassination . . . —you will perhaps hear of me no more.[2]

I am surprised that the wretch who attacked me has not been heard of. Surely the inquiries have not been sufficiently general, or particular? Mr. Nanney requests that you will order that some boards should be nailed against the broken window at Tanyrallt. We are in immediate want of money.[3]

We expect to be there [Dublin] on the 8th. You shall then hear the detail of our distresses. The ball of the assassins [sic] pistol (he fired at me twice) penetrated my night gown and pierced the wainscot. He is yet undiscovered though not unsuspected as you will learn from my next.[4]

The third account is in a letter from Shelley's wife Harriet written a fortnight after the event:

Mr. S. promised you a recital of the horrible events that caused us to leave Wales. I have undertaken the task, as I wish to spare him, in the present nervous state of his health, every [sic] thing that can recall to his mind the horrors of that night, which I will relate.

On Friday night, the 26th of February, we retired to bed between ten and eleven o'clock. We had been in bed about half an hour, when Mr. S. heard a noise proceeding from one of the parlours. He immediately went downstairs with two pistols, which he had loaded that night, expecting to have occasion for them. He went into the billiard room, where he heard footsteps retreating. He followed into an [sic] other little room, which was called an office. He there saw a man in the act of quitting the room through a glass window which opens into the shrubbery. The man fired at Mr. S., which he avoided. Bysshe then fired, but it flashed in the pan. The man then knocked Bysshe down, and they struggled on the ground. Bysshe then fired his second pistol, which he thought wounded him in the shoulder, as he uttered a shriek and got

[1] Mrs. William's account (1860) from recollection of her husband's conversation in 1820 and the succeeding years. The original sketch has been lost, but a copy was made and is reproduced here as published in the *Century Magazine*, October, 1905, by permission of Appleton-Century-Crofts, Inc.
[2] Shelley to Hookham, his publisher, the day after or within a few days.
[3] Shelley to Williams, within two or three days.
[4] Shelley to Hookham, 6 March, 1813.

up, when he said these words: By God. I will be revenged! I will murder your wife. I will ravish your sister. By God. I will be revenged. He then fled—as we hoped for the night. Our servants were not gone to bed, but were just going, when this horrible affair happened. This was about eleven o'clock. We all assembled in the parlour, where we remained for two hours. Mr. S. then advised us to retire, thinking it impossible he would make a second attack. We left Bysshe and our manservant, who only arrived that day, and who knew nothing of the house, to sit up. I had been in bed three hours, when I heard a pistol go off. I immediately ran down stairs, when I perceived that Bysshe's flannel gown had been shot through, and the window curtain. Bysshe had sent Daniel to see what hour it was, when he heard a noise at the window. He went there, and a man thrust his arm through the glass and fired at him. Thank Heaven! the ball went through his gown and he remained unhurt, Mr. S. happened to stand sideways; had he stood fronting, the ball must have killed him. Bysshe fired his pistol, but it would not go off. He then aimed a blow at him with an old sword which we found in the house. The assassin attempted to get the sword from him, and just as he was pulling it away Dan rushed into the room, when he made his escape.

This was at four in the morning. It had been a most dreadful night; the wind was as loud as thunder, and the rain descended in torrents. Nothing has been heard of him; and we have reason to believe it was no stranger, as there was a man of the name of Leeson, who the next morning that it happened went and told the shopkeepers of Tremadoc that it was a tale of Mr. Shelley's to impose upon them, that he might leave the country without paying his bills. This they believed, and none of them attempted to do anything towards his discovery.

We left Tanyrallt on Saturday. . . .[1]

Examination of the scene next day showed certain physical traces of the events of the night, in addition to the sketch. A window, apparently of the drawing-room, was broken; 'the grass on the lawn appeared to have been much trampled and rolled on, but there were no footprints on the wet ground, except between the beaten spot and the window; and the impression of the ball on the wainscot showed that the pistol had been fired towards the window, and not from it.'

The affair has been viewed, in a cycle which has continued till the present, as an hallucinatory experience, as a performance deliberately

---

[1] Harriet Shelley to Hookham, 12 March, 1813.

staged (though perhaps embroidered with some exuberance of fantasy not altogether under conscious control) to provide a plausible excuse to escape financial and other difficulties at Tremadoc, and as a genuine attack. The authors of the two most thorough studies made of Shelley in the last twenty years find the evidence against a genuine attack 'cumulatively conclusive'; there remain delusion and fraud. Of these, I find delusion by far the more probable.

## I

I have lately examined some of the accounts of Shelley's life and also his poems, and I find they illustrate a conclusion which I had already formed from experience and reading: that adoring narcissism, double-going and suicide are three stages in, or aspects of, a unified process.

By adoring narcissism I mean a state in which the subject is constantly impelled to gaze at his own image in reflecting surfaces. At first he does so with serene admiration. Later, with mouth slackly open and eyes of longing sadness he yearns towards the image, imagining himself by turns as his own future wife standing before him in submissive love and as his future self comforting her with a tender and passionless embrace. Later still he looks at his solemn image with increasingly puzzled anxiety, expressed in the unspoken or whispered words: 'Who am I?', 'What am I?', or even 'What are you?' At dusk his features may seem to have a smooth or haggard darkness, an evil, feline expression. Later, as he stands with bent head before his motionless reflection, it may at last come to seem a mere thing with which he feels hardly any identity. This is almost the final state to which adoring narcissism may progress, namely the condition of 'mirror-blindness' where the subject 'cannot see himself in a mirror' or 'I see something, but it's not myself'.

Interspersed with stages of anxiety and despair in relation to the image, are periods when the subjects feels himself a 'lovely lad' as he gazes for minutes into the glass, wearing—with a sense of charm and virtue—a satyr-like smile. When the mood is more intense, a fiercer smile appears, with the lower jaw forced open against the tension of the lips and the eyes widened.

In the anxiety phase, a strong sense of uneasiness, accompanied by a painful feeling of isolation, may be felt towards an image reflected against the night in the window of a lighted room or of a train in which one is travelling. In ecstatic self-contemplation, however, an unexpected encounter with one's own image, especially in a full-length mirror, produces an inward thrill lending brilliance to the figure.

103

An impulse to use two mirrors to obtain a view of oneself as others see one, from behind or in profile, arises in the development of this narcissistic state. The aim here (as it presents itself to consciousness) is to gain reassurance that there is nothing in one's appearance to lack confidence about. The profile seen in this way may suddenly—perhaps when the smile I have described is put on—come to have something feral about it, which at once strips away the illusive sense of charm and makes mirror-gazing disagreeable for a time.

Finally, there may appear impulses to injure or destroy the image. The mirror may be broken because the subject 'cannot bear the sight of himself'; or the impulse may be to see the image injured by inflicting injury on one's self—a fascination with how the image would look if such and such a thing were done to it.

Other aspects of narcissism, for example the preference for monotone or nondescript clothing, 'histrionic' tendencies and feelings toward one's shadow, can be left out of account for the present purpose, for which, however, one frequent accompaniment requires description. For the subject of adoring narcissism will also undergo, from early in life, a series of passionate, though often distant, adorations for others of like appearance and usually of the same sex, but more delicate, brilliant, youthful. Devotion for this person, for whom no sacrifice would be inconceivable, seems to link his life with one's own. The strength of these emotions, which may extend to the Biblical 'yearning of the bowels', may become so great as to make the actual company of the hero or heroine uncomfortable or insupportable to the worshipper; he will then seek to express himself in wandering where destiny will surely—it is at once hoped and feared—bring about an encounter charged with meaning. He hopes eagerly to find in this other a sharer of his intellectual aspirations and his personal view of life. If this hope founders, its place will be taken not by a determination to persuade, but by a tongue-tied emptiness. When he has the object of adoration in sight, but is not in his company, his eyes may be riveted to the other's face, while he wears the satyr's smile. There may come to his mind, on the theme of doing the other some great service, a scene in which he imagines coming upon the other preparing to kill himself and disuades and comforts him, convincing him that, with himself beside him, life cannot be without meaning; this thought is more likely to appear if suicides have occurred in the environment he shares with the other.

No one, I think, who has experienced the Narcissus-state and doublegoing could doubt the connection between them. For doublegoing is seeing, awake or dreaming, a phantasm of oneself; or, in a more extended sense, visualising a second self or harbouring such a figure as an un-realized image. Such a figure is perceived in the mind as a distinct second person whose intention and will one can only guess. Usually the figure is marked with one's own appearance, which may, however, be exaggerated in one direction or another. I call this figure a 'mee', a term more convenient and less ambiguous than the usual 'Doppelgänger'; I derive it from the spontaneous ejaculation in the astonishment of the first encounter.

Shelley saw a mee twice a few days before his death, once waking and once in a sleepwalking dream. Goethe met his mee on his way home from a visit to Friederike Brion. Maupassant's mee came and sat opposite him. As Axel Munthe described the incident:

He often used to rush up the steps of Avenue deVilliers to sit down in a corner of my room looking at me in silence with that morbid fixity of his eyes I knew so well. Often he used to stand for minutes staring at himself in the mirror over the mantelpiece as if he was looking at a stranger. One day he told me that while he was sitting at his writing-table hard at work on his new novel he had been greatly surprised to see a stranger enter his study notwithstanding the severe vigilance of his valet. The stranger had sat down opposite him at the writing-table and began to dictate to him what he was about to write. He was just going to ring for François to have him turned out when he saw to his horror that the stranger was himself.

Visualizations or fantasies of the mee appear to develop in two stages. First, one transports oneself into the identity of an anonymous observer of oneself who watches from a little distance away. Later, without quitting one's own person, one sees a duplicate of oneself acting independently.

I dreamed that in a restaurant, in whose mirrored wall I had once in reality companioned my reflection and been alone with him though I was one of a party, I saw a mee, wearing my usual clothing, seated with his back towards me at a table against the far wall. He raised a revolver in his right hand towards his head; instantly I was sitting where I had seen the mee, a revolver in my right hand (the mee here was more than a simple mirror-image, for left and right were not reversed); I put the muzzle to my right temple, where I felt it cold and round. I believe I then pressed the trigger; at all events, the dream ended abruptly.

On another occasion I dreamed I was looking down from a right-hand box of a theatre on the bare boards of a harshly lighted stage. I was conscious of no other audience. I felt a strong anxiety directed towards the lower edges of the grey or black hangings surrounding the stage. A grim, lank-haired figure, drably clad, the shape of his head and features my own, but his expression almost unrecognizably sombre and haggard, stood in the centre of the stage mouthing wordless threats. Another figure leapt from the curtains and struck him down from behind; as he did so, several others ran out from under the curtains and rushed to and fro at the back of the stage. At the same moment, it was I who stood on the stage where the evil mee had stood, in guilt and terror, but whether for murder done by me or to be done upon me I did not know. I knew, without having expressly seen it, that the weapon was a knife, but I remember neither corpse nor blood and dared not look down. Where I had first been was above and to the left of where I now stood. Had I been the leaping, striking figure? Was I now that figure triumphant or his victim about to fall?

These episodes formed part of a series of dreams in which a mee often appeared to me. Previously I had seldom dreamed, but the series began abruptly at a time when, having passed through the development of adoring narcissism with almost all the features I have described, I was subject to a powerful impulse to suicide, the threat of which was perceived by others before I recognized it myself.

Occasionally it may be recorded that a literary presentation of double-going took its rise from a dream remembered by the author. Stevenson's account of the dream episodes which gave him the essence of *Dr. Jekyll and Mr. Hyde* and his long preoccupation with the theme of 'a fellow who was two fellows' suggest that the figure of Hyde was, in its first conception, an evil mee. In any event, one cannot suppose an essential difference between dream doublegoing and autoscopic delusion; they are merely two levels of presentation of the same phenomenon.

Few if any literary works exhibit *all* the principal features of narcissism, doublegoing, and suicide. Many features of narcissism do not lend themselves to embodiment in a story, which as a rule require the interplay of separate characters. It is easier to find instances of authors whose life and works, taken as a whole, display such connections: Shelley was one such, Poe another, Maupassant a third.

Maupassant's *The Horla* starts with the diarist seeing, from the garden of his white house, a white Brazilian schooner being towed up the lower

Seine. A few days later he becomes uneasy and has a repeated dream in which, while he 'feels and sees' he is asleep, some one comes up, looks at him, kneels upon him and tries to strangle him. In vain he struggles to shout, move or throw off his assailant. He awakes, alone. Walking in the forest one day, he is suddenly terrified that someone is following close at his heels. He whirls around—but is alone.

Several nights later he finds that someone is drinking from the water-bottle at his bedside and by an elaborate experiment convinces himself that it is not he but another. In Paris an encounter with hypnotism suggests to him the possession of one's soul by another will. Back home, an unseen hand plucks a rose beside him as he walks in his garden. He feels someone always near him, watching, entering into his being, dominating his will. One evening he sees the pages of a book turn as if the book is being read as it lies on a table before his empty chair. He leaps toward the chair, but it overturns as the invisible occupant escapes through the window, leaving the room in confusion.

He reads about a strange madness raging in Brazil—a haunting by invisible presences—and he connects this with the white Brazilian schooner, his own white house, and the being who haunts *him* and for whom the generic name 'Horla' comes into his mind, as though borne faintly on a wind from a world beyond. The Horla is to supplant man as lord of creation, dominating man by his will, just as man dominates the beasts by his superior intellect. But sometimes beasts rebel. . . . He feels the Horla within him, becoming his soul; he will kill him.

One night he sits writing in his brilliantly lighted bedroom when suddenly the Horla is reading over his shoulder. He rises and turns, with hands outstretched to slay his persecutor, when he sees, empty of all reflection, clear and full of light, the full-length mirror before which he daily shaves and dresses and in which it is his habit to survey himself, from head to foot, every time he goes past it. He stands rooted to the spot, not daring to leap upon the invisible being whose substance, he supposes, has absorbed his image. Little by little, the image returns as though emerging from a mist, which drifts away from left to right. He conceives the plan of enticing the Horla into his room, locking him in, and then burning down the house. He has his room specially barred and locks himself in with the Horla, whom he feels moving around the room in alarm. He backs carefully out through the just sufficiently open door, locks it behind him, sets fire to the house and watches it burn. He is sure the Horla is dead—but then he has a sudden, overwhelming doubt: could fire harm insubstantial nature? So the Horla is still alive! His sole recourse, he suddenly concludes, is to kill himself.

*William Wilson* by Poe is the story, told in the first person, of an evil liver who, from schooldays, is repeatedly shamed and unmasked by an identical namesake, unlike him only in having no speaking voice, only a whisper. At school the narrator is intimate with his double, yet feels an anxious sense of inferior rivalry, 'some petulant animosity, which was not yet hatred, some esteem, more respect, much fear, with a world of uneasy curiosity'. He resents his rival's moral tutelage and seeks, with partial success, to wound and humiliate him. The double retaliates by a precise mimicry, which is, however, noticed only by the narrator who, incidentally senses having known his double before.

One night, intent on making his rival 'feel the whole extent of the malice' with which he is imbued, he goes to his rival's room. But as he gazes down at the sleeping face of his intended victim, he is so terrified by the identity of appearance which is borne in upon him that he flees.

The narrator passes to a life of profligate folly as 'a student at Eton', where the second Wilson appears, clothed precisely as the narrator, whispers their shared name and, with a gesture of admonition, disappears. The narrator's subsequent career at Oxford, where he 'added no brief appendix to the long catalogue of vices then usual in the most dissolute university of Europe', ends when the second Wilson unmasks him cheating at cards. Time and again, never showing his face, the second Wilson intervenes at the critical moment, always on the side of righteousness.

At length the narrator, his feelings heightened by alcohol, resolves to be subject no longer to the will of his corrector. When the second Wilson seeks to frustrate an amorous design of the narrator at a masked ball, he drags him into a small room, forces a swordfight, and plunges his sword again and again into his double. Someone tries the door and the narrator turns to latch it. When he turns round again it seems for a moment that there is a large mirror at the far end of the room, in which, as he walks towards it, his own image, fatally wounded, advances to meet him. But it is his rival who totters there, never more exactly his counterpart, his face, unmasked, now seen at last, his voice no longer a whisper, so that the narrator might fancy that he himself is speaking as his rival says:

You have conquered, and I yield. Yet henceforward art thou also dead—dead to the World, to Heaven, and to Hope! In me didst thou exist—and, in my death, see by this image, which is thine own, how utterly thou hast murdered thyself.

## II

Now, if it is allowed that narcissism and doublegoing are allied and that suicide is bound up with them, and that where these tendencies occur together, the subject of them may experience incompletely realized manifestations of doublegoing, then there are reasons for thinking that Shelley's opponent at Tanyrallt was his own image seen in the window and that the sketch he drew was of his mee.

Shelley was narcissistic. I have found no record of a habit of looking too much in mirrors, but there are evidences in his life and writings that the mirror-world and his own likeness had great attraction for him. His adoring, dependent love for his sister Elizabeth, so like him in looks, and whom he wished to find or make so like him in ideas, may have had a narcissistic basis. He described often and with delight the still, clean, fairer world that lies reflected in unruffled pools and streams (see *The Recollection*, IV; *Prometheus Unbound*, Act III, Scene III; *The Cloud*, IV; *Evening—Ponte a Mare, Pisa*, iii; *Ode to Liberty*, VI; *The Sensitive Plant*, Part I, v; *Witch of Atlas*, LIX). Sometimes he used a human metaphor in describing the reflections of natural objects (see *Alastor*). He described, like one who has himself experienced it, a young poet's contemplation of his own reflection (see *Alastor*). He gives a lifelike account of brooding upon a haggard-seeming image, such as characterises the anxiety phase of narcissism:

> I saw my countenance reflected there;—
> And then my youth fell on me like a wind
> Descending on still waters—my thin hair
> Was prematurely grey, my face was lined
> With channels, such as suffering leaves behind,
> Not age;
>
> *Revolt of Islam*, IV, xxix

He speaks of an impulse to mirror gazing coming with the spring:
> How many a one, though none be near to love,
> Loves then the shade of his own soul, half seen
> In any mirror—
>
> *Prince Athanase*, Fragment III

110

Shelley was a doublegoer. In the last days of his life he encountered his mee once while awake (it asked, 'How long do you mean to be content?') and once in a sleep-walking dream in which he saw the mee strangling his second wife Mary. He introduced his own image into *Adonais*, a lament not for Keats alone, but for himself supposed dead (*Adonais*, XXXI – XXXIV). He described dream-doublegoing (*Revolt of Islam*, Canto III, xxiii). He visualized a phantom counterpart of the whole world and all its creatures (*Prometheus Unbound*, Act I). In a picture of human life dissolving in famine and plague and thirst he associated doublegoing with suicide:

> It was not thirst but madness! Many saw
> Their own lean image everywhere; it went
> A ghastlier self beside them, till the awe
> Of that dread sight to self-destruction sent
> Those shrieking victims;
> *Revolt of Islam*, Canto X, xxii

> Thine own soul still is true to thee,
> But changed to a foul fiend through misery.

> This fiend, whose ghastly presence ever
> Beside thee like thy shadow hangs,
> Dream not to chase;—the mad endeavour
> Would scrouge thee to severer pangs.
> Be as thou art. Thy settled fate,
> Dark as it is, all change would aggravate.
> From '*Oh! there are spirits in the air*'

Sometimes the divine female in whose shape he symbolized Intellectual Beauty has adjuncts which suggest that she is, in part at least, a mee:

> He dreamed a veiled maid
> Sate near him, talking in low solemn tones.
> Her voice was like the voice of his own soul
> Heard in the calm of thought;
> *Alastor*

In many of his longer poems he portrayed himself as seen by another. In *Julian and Maddalo*, both the narrator, Julian, and the Madman, whom Maddalo (Byron) takes him to see, are Shelley. In the preface to the poem Shelley pays to Julian's character, as to another's, a tribute of approval not concealed by mild depreciation. In a long monologue in which, forgetting that he is supposed to be talking, the Madman speaks of his words flowing 'from his pen', Shelley pours out his own distresses. The Madman tells how he is held back from suicide only by the desire not to cause pain to one once dearly loved, whom he feels scorns and wronged him.

These instances belong to the years from 1815. *Queen Mab*, which Shelley finished and largely wrote at Tanyrallt during the winter of 1812–13, suggests that at that time doublegoing in himself had reached his conscious thoughts in an imaginative shape. A 'Fairy Queen' of magical powers carries away the 'Soul' or 'Spirit' of a sleeping young woman into the vastness of space and from there shows it a vision of the world, past, present and to come.

Shelley was suicidal. He spoke often of suicide, wrote of it in his letters and poems, more than once procured poison or sought to procure it, tried to kill himself at least once (in the stormy days before his elopement with Mary Woolstonecraft) and met a death which, if not half-sought, was at least half-desired.

## III

It is the sketch itself, however, which most clearly bears the stamp of narcissism and doublegoing. The figure has, I think, a certain quality of 'doubleness'. If the lines forming the square are ignored, there is the suggestion of a powerful creature, its jaws ferociously agape, prancing towards its right, while over its shoulder looks a grinning second head. With the lines, one sees a demon facing forwards, looking round from behind something on which a bestial profile is inexplicably cast.

The expression and position of the face, appearing round an edge, are narcissistic. The broad, curving grin, with jaw forced down and lips drawn back to expose the teeth, and the widely opened eyes constitute the expression of fierce narcissism, that more intense form of the satyr's smile of self-adoration which I noted earlier.

I mentioned that one manifestation of narcissism is to get views as-others-see-me of oneself. One such view is that from behind. To obtain it the subject stands with his back to a large mirror, holds a hand mirror up in front of him, and looks at the reflection in it of the large mirror. The hand mirror must be held somewhat to one side—let us say to the right, as would be most usual. Since the subject wishes to see himself as he is seen by others, he holds his head facing directly forwards so that he sees the back of it full, probably tilting his head slightly to the right and a little downwards.

Now, looking into the hand mirror in this posture, the subject sees a reflected view from behind of his own figure; the figure's head is tilted to the right and a little downwards and in its right hand it holds a hand mirror; looking at this twice-reflected image of the hand mirror (the eyes must be strongly rotated to the right) the subjects sees reflected again in it his own face, full or nearly so, tilted to its left and slightly forwards, its lower right hand part invisible beyond the edge of the hand mirror's reflection, the eyes rolled strongly to their left and slightly upwards. If the eyes are then widened and a grin made, a disconcertingly 'diabolical' effect results, lacking only the narcissistic curvature of the lips to be precisely what Shelley drew.

That the square in the upper left of the picture represents a plane surface may be deduced from its relation to the face and upper part of the body of the main figure. It is probably a mirror or reflecting surface, perhaps an open casement window. It may be objected that the feral face in it is the 'devil's' face, not the profile which should be within the mirror, and that the full face, in order to cast a reflection in profile into a mirror, should be in front of and not behind the mirror. That it is not so certainly detracts from an ideal concurrence between the sketch and the explanation I have offered. But a certain composite quality must be allowed to the sketch; indeed, close examination shows it was drawn in two stages: first the complete figure in profile, faint and tentative, then the square outline with the strongly drawn grinning face peering round it. The pair of fainter lines, forming a sharp curve beside the visible left-hand corner of the grin, mark the outline of the back of the head of the complete figure first drawn in profile. The faint lines beneath the left eye and across the brow of the grinning face probably belong to the profile figure, forming part of a projection from the head, less precise in shape than the 'horns' and snake.

Now it is curious that Shelley's pistol twice failed to go off immediately after his assailant had fired at him; had he himself already fired it? The threat uttered by the assailant to murder Shelley's wife foreshadows the action of the mee which at Casa Magni he saw strangling his second wife.

When Shelley *went to the window,* may he not have thrust his own pistol through the glass from inside and seen his reflection do the same from outside? The swordfight through the broken window could, without difficulty, have been a most lifelike contest with a mirror image, and in such a contest through a hole in a reflecting surface, the image would appear to be struggling to pull the sword away from one's grasp by gripping it at the hilt. As to the shot through the nightgown and the curtain, may not that have been a token act of self-slaughter before a mirror, that is, before the window?

This explanation of the incident at Tanyrallt is dependent on there having been some illumination in the room where the window was broken, since without that the window could not have acted as a mirror. We know it was a dark night, so a comparatively weak source of light would have been enough. It might seem imprudent for anyone expecting to be shot at to sit up in a lighted room, but it is not impossible that Shelley did so, perhaps with the curtains drawn, perhaps out of sight from the window, perhaps without these precautions; for it is not impossible amid so many improbabilities and inconsistencies that there should have been one more.

*W. H. McCulloch*

For the lineal procedure of individual awareness, Joyce, in his last work, substituted an everyway roundabout with intrusions from above and below. For those locked in the metallic and rectilinear embrace of the printed page Joyce appears as a surrealist magician or clown. But his optophone principle in art provides the key for future literary and social education. The optophone is an instrument for turning images into sounds. Surrounded by a vast new imagery, technological man has yet to learn how to interpret this imagery verbally or socially. Until he learns its language it will continue to act on him like the new liquid meat tenderizers. In the *Wake* Joyce provided the sounds which are the magic key to the new technological visual environment. More than that, these sounds are both acoustically and semantically continuous with the linguistic activity of the race. The *Wake* may take a few months to get acquainted with, but it represents a great short-out to the encyclopedic arts and sciences of our century. It is the sheer quantity of information which has alienated us from political and social reality. The large city isolates the individual citizen, but the multi-cultural perspectives of the press have isolated the human spirit itself from any milieu.

A decisive instance of this isolation is the popular sleuth of detective fiction. Whether it be Holmes or Marlowe the sleuth is an alienated man, but he is one who uses the communication networks of the metropolis as a kind of musical instrument. The appeal of detective stories is not least in the power of the sleuth to control the city as an instrument of expression. He turns the city into poetry.

What Joyce has shown us is how to do for the whole of existence what the sleuth does with the keyboard of the city. Today we are compelled by the quantity of available social and political facts to learn a new visual language for swiftly mastering the inner dynamics by the outer carapace of facts.

Perhaps nothing more bespeaks the hypnotic and irrational pressure of the book-page than the scant attention it has received as a form. In the 16th century it required an effort to read print comparable to the effort today exerted to master symphonic scores or mathematical pictograms. Moreover a passage of Greene, Lyly, or Nashe is not prose in the 18th or 19th century sense. The focus of attention has to be readjusted for changes of tone and attitude in every sentence. Print had not yet imposed its massive mechanical weight to level off the oral and colloquial features of prose. Even punctuation was not for the reading eye but the speaking voice—a fact lost on the 19th century editors of Shakespeare. The triumphs of 20th century editing of Shakespeare have mainly consisted in abandoning the habits of rigid perspective induced by three centuries of print-hypnosis. Print is an ill master for those who are unaware of the precise nature and scope of its power. The printed word is no longer a means of testing reality. *Caveat emptor.*

The modern movie camera resembles Elizabethan prose in its demands of agility and multiple mental focus. *Vogue* recently printed an essay by an English novelist who confessed that he was mostly unable to follow the development of movie narrative and characterization and that he had to rely on his less bookish wife to interpret the action to him.

Rosamond Tuve in a recent book on George Herbert makes it her theme that the metaphysical poets, so congenial to our century, typically found their novel effects in the transfer of traditional pictorial imagery to the new printed page. Hers is no friendly analysis. In 1600 print was in the ascendant and the old pictorial 'Bibles of the Poor', painted cloths, dumb shows and popular spectacles were in decline. Today the reverse process obtains. At the equilibrium point in these two processes the seventeenth century metaphysical poets shot up into favorable view once more. We shared with them for twenty years a bi-focal vision of the interfusion of two media.

At the end of the 18th century Whiter, an Anglican clergyman, anticipated much 20th century critical appreciation of Shakespeare by studying the imagery of his plays. One of his observations was that Shakespeare in *Antony and Cleopatra* or *The Tempest*, for example, brought verbally to the ordinary man the gorgeous scenic virtuosities of the Jacobean court masque.

In *Spirit of the Age* (1825) William Hazlitt summed up a century of romantic revolt and experiment in his comments on the relation between books and painting:

> Book-learning, the accumulation of wordy common-places, the gaudy pretensions of poetical fiction, had enfeebled and perverted our eye for nature. The study of the fine arts, which came into fashion about forty years ago, and was then first considered as a polite accomplishment, would tend imperceptibly to restore it. Painting is essentially an imitative art; it cannot subsist for a moment on empty generalities: the critic, therefore, who had been used to this sort of substantial entertainment, would be disposed to read poetry with the eye of a connoisseur, would be little captivated with smooth, polished, unmeaning periods, and would turn with double eagerness and relish to the force and precision of individual details, transferred, as it were, to the page from the canvas. Thus an admirer of Teniers or Hobbima might think little of the pastoral sketches of Pope or Goldsmith; even Thomson describes not so much the naked object as what he sees in his mind's eye, surrounded and glowing with the mild, bland, genial vapours of his brain:—but the adept in Dutch interiors . . . must find in Mr. Crabbe a man after his own heart. He is the very thing itself; he paints in words instead of colours. . . . All the rest might be found in a newspaper, an old magazine, or a county-register.

George Crabbe was Lord Tennyson's favorite narrative poet. And the early Tennyson was a radical experimenter in picturesque painting technique. It may well have been Arnold whose criticism turned English literary attention away for a few decades from an inclusive consciousness of the techniques in the arts. From Chaucer to Tennyson it would be hard to find a poet who was not an eager student of the non-literary culture of his own day. But since English became a University subject (in the past fifty years or less) it has been customary not only to study poetry and letters without reference to technique and effect but in isolation from the other arts and sciences. It has been observed that any crisis in a culture, an organization, or a person calls for a great extension of the internal and external modes of communication. Precisely the reverse of this has occurred in the area of book-culture today.

117

This fact explains a good deal of the current helplessness in literary circles with regard to illiteracy and the new media. The study of the classics earlier disappeared in the same fashion. Writing in *Encounter* (April, 1954), Auden discusses 'The Word and the Machine'. Poets today, he says, envy 'not the rich or the powerful but the scientists, doctors, machine designers, etc., for whose happiness our age seems designed as earlier ages were designed for great landowners, for these people enjoy the satisfaction both of meaningful work and of an unequivocal social position. When I am in the company of scientists, I feel like a curate who has strayed into a drawing-room full of dukes.'

A few years before, Mr. Auden's colleague Stephen Spender was wanly asking why, when he met a communist, did he feel so small? Both having failed in the thirties to find a satisfactory lyrical idiom to glorify the machine might now unite in the matter of dukes. Or doesn't it matter that the machine has now brought English noblemen to the pass of purveying home-made jam at the roadside? The fact of the matter is that Mr. Auden typifies our current failure to examine the forms of technology, past and present, as art forms. He concludes his essay:

Is there something in the essential natures of the machine and the Word which makes them incompatible, so that at the slightest contact with the former the Word turns into lifeless words? Is even the mechanical printing press, but for which I would never have been able to read the books that formed my life, nor for that matter be writing this article now, an evil? Sometimes I have an uneasy suspicion that it is.

After four centuries of uncritical ebullience and commercial log-rolling it would seem to be safe to have a suspicion about the effects of print. Especially now that print has been knocked off its pedestal by other media. But it is still not too late to save some of the qualities of mind fostered by the printed page, provided we are prepared to note exactly what the limits of those qualities are and have been. Study of pre-literate societies and manuscript cultures can give excellent indications of the merits and defects of book-culture. These in co-ordination with music and painting as technical forms of managing experience can in turn provide excellent clues for understanding the new pictorial media.

Siegfrid Giedion has given exact procedures for how the modern painter or poet should conduct himself in the company of scientists: Adopt and adapt their discoveries to the uses of art. Why leave this solely to the distortions of the industrialist? Newton revolutionized the techniques of poetry and painting. Joyce encompasses Einstein but extends his pictographic formula to the entire world of language and consciousness. The tendency of the challengingly new to revoke and reenforce ancient disciplines never appeared more strikingly than in Joyce. Literature may have come to an end in 1870 but poetic, rhetoric and metaphysic have come increasingly alive since then.

One reason why the literate English world is so helpless in the presence of the new media is perhaps owing to England's having been so backward in 1500. The Wars of the Roses had delayed the impact of the Renaissance. In England alone that impact coincided with the arrival of the printing press. The cultural lop-sidedness of a literary monopoly appears even more strikingly in New England in the 17th century. But it needs to be stressed that printed culture is itself a triumph of the machine. And book-culture in England and America was *in its very format* a great incentive to the mechanization of society. The book-page is the first mass-produced machine product. This fact is as obvious to men of Mediterranean culture as the fact that backward communities are the oral libraries of the world's ancient cultures is obvious to archaeologists. Why should it be surprising that the most literate societies are the most mechanized? Why should literate men bemoan the mechanization of speech and gesture (radio and television) when it is precisely the mechanization of writing that made this development possible? Would it be too much to suggest that universal literacy is unfriendly to critical perception? With 25,000 and more new titles in English each year who is to note the significant, let alone 'the best that has been thought and said in the world'?

It is the almost total coverage of the globe in time and space that has rendered the book an increasingly obsolete form of communication. The slow movement of the eye along lines of type, the slow procession of items organized by the mind to fit into these endless horizontal columns, these procedures can't stand up to the pressures of instantaneous coverage of the earth.

The American Revolution occurred just when the newspaper was sufficiently a reality to be changing and extending surface transport. The American Government was the first to be founded on the concept of public opinion. Such a concept still seems bizarre in Canada. It was the new medium not of the book but the press which shaped the U.S.A. And this creates a political crisis with the passing of the press into the entertainment limbo, and with the rise of TV as a political shaper. But it has also been the typical mistake of literate cultures to regard entertainment as non-political. Russia made no such slip.

What is to be expected in the mainly non-literate India and China, countries which are in a position to by-pass literacy and proceed at once with radio and TV? These countries represent high cultures which are almost entirely oral and pictographic. Their rapport with TV far exceeds our own. If the new medium of the press gave a radical imprint to American politics, how much more might the new medium of TV be ordained to shape power patterns in the Orient? Should this occur, our own political structures, tied to print, would be quite unable to catch up. Russia provides some hints for this process. Enjoying the end products of our technology as regards industry, press, radio, and movie, it assumed them at a pre-industrial point in its own development, just as the Orient is in a position to assume end-products of an even later stage of our development into an even earlier stage of its own. The dream-character of movie and TV realism would seem to be connaturally adjusted to 'the dreaming East'. The giant djinns of oriental fancy are pygmy-like in size and power compared even with the superhuman dimensions conferred by our own daily press and weekly magazines on nobody in particular. But even more, movie and TV have the almost uncontrollable power of inflating the most casually selected persons into million horse-powered entities. Men trained in book-culture are slow to assess these facts. Yet they will admit that even books, by and large, have been written by their reading publics. Authors have always been shaped by their potential publics.

But the new media are not 'authored' by single individuals any more than a modern newspaper. As the public of the new media increases the 'author' staff increases. Scott or Dickens could net a nation. But no single writer today can encompass more than a fragment of the available attention of the public. The media have transformed the public in many ways and the public goes on transforming the techniques and consciousness of the authors who would master it. The man who has something to say is the man who has mastered some segment of public awareness. He is capable of lighting up some dim, fusty corner of embryonic social consciousness. Formerly an author could do this by introspection, when he was essentially a member of society. Today when it is no longer possible to be sure of what being a member of society may involve, the 'author' has to bestir himself as much as any pollster. He lives in an unknown world of strange new components and effects.

In *Explorations Two* it was suggested that the new situation in the modern class-room is that the adolescent today does not need information. He is hopelessly overloaded with messages from the urban environment. The class-room no longer need typically perform the function of providing facts. It must above all provide techniques of recognition and discrimination. Reality-testing can no longer follow the linear, factual recital or statistical pattern. There is far too much reality for that. We are obliged to deal with reality in constellations and clusters or not at all. If politics and the citizen are to survive the new media, we must alter our entire sighting and range-finding apparatus, which is still oriented to the printed page alone.

*Marshall McLuhan*

'Human behaviour' is not an easy subject to define concretely. Conventionally, it has been apportioned among the sciences somewhat as a primitive hunter distributes the pieces of an animal he has killed: a haunch here, a shoulder there, the entrails to this person, and the brains to that, without any particular regard to the functional anatomy of the organism as a whole; some parts of the animal are simply lost or thrown away. Behavioural scientists consequently have had some difficulty in seeing either how their own particular segments work or how the whole animal works, and have not done a very satisfying job of putting the pieces back together again; indeed, the results of re-synthesis sometimes are so monstrous that one wonders if such a creature could *ever* have existed, since certain organs are so misconstrued as to become logically incompatible with the rest of the animal. It is worse than a group of blind men trying to *identify* an elephant; it is more like a group of blind men trying to *make* an elephant out of the dismembered pieces of a hippopotamus.

Now there is an expectation, in some quarters, of the imminent birth of a new scientific discipline, which shall in several of its features resemble the partial and separate (but 'blind') studies of human behaviour from which it is descended, but which at the same time shall possess its own distinctive character and lineaments. This new science of human behaviour, scion of anthropology, sociology, history, psychology, and psychiatry, with economics, political science, human biology, mathematics, and the humanities as collateral relatives, is to 'integrate' the concepts, theories, and data of its ancestral disciplines. Heir of the older sciences, it will infuse its inheritance with a new life and vigour, and make theories of learning, facts of history, patterns of culture, and principles of psychodynamics mutually supporting organs in a well-organized, new theoretical-empirical system.

Labour pains have several times been reported, and a corps of eager midwives is standing ready to assist. For some years the Institute of Human Relations at Yale University has been struggling to bring forth this child; a representative of the organization has even proposed a patronymic nickname—'lesocupethy', standing for 'learning, society, culture, personality, and theory'—and the Institute has published several 'Behavior Science' outlines and monographs. The *accouchement* at Yale was followed by *couvade* symptoms on other campuses: at Harvard, for instance, where anthropologists, sociologists, and social and clinical psychologists bedded down in the Department of Social Relations; at the University of Pennsylvania, where an interest in interdisciplinary studies has brought together certain historians, sociologists, psychiatrists, anthropologists, and psychologists under the sign of the 'Behavioral Research Council'; at Chicago, where a faculty seminar group has been working to develop a general theory of behaviour; and in various other interdisciplinary divisions, committees, and research projects, too numerous to list, at universities and foundations all over the United States and Canada.

OBSTACLES

*Provincialism.* Perhaps the outstanding—and certainly the most obvious—obstacle in the way of a science of human behaviour, is organized provincialism among behavioural scientists. In its most extreme form of intellectual expression it takes the shape of 'closed systems': in assertions that culture can only be explained in terms of culture, or that social facts can only be determined by other social facts, or that anthropological techniques are inapplicable to large and complex civilized societies because anthropologists study small and simple primitive societies, or that findings in abnormal psychology cannot be extended to normal people, and so on. Such sentiments are, unhappily, useful for rationalizing the understandable but deleterious proposition that the aim of a science

123

is the mutual job-promotion of the scientists rather than the extension of knowledge. Where such sentiments prevail, a covert anxiety is apt to surround any effort to enlarge the scope of a discipline to include, or to accept, other material or viewpoints than those traditionally its own, and the atmosphere can degenerate to that of an association of tradesmen devoted to the 'Fair Trade' peddling of their products.

*The Youth Complex.* We social scientists are perpetually excusing our real and fancied insufficiencies by asserting that ours is a very 'young' science; that in our present 'stage' we may be awkward, but that we are doing just what we should be doing now (i.e., either collecting a stockpile of facts, or groping toward a theory of something or other), and that in the next stage 'immaturity' will be replaced by a remarkable fruition.

Actually, the behavioural sciences are not really young at all any more; I suspect that we are in fact almost as old as scientific chemistry, physics, and biology. We maintain the fiction of our youth by ignoring as 'unscientific' everything done before certain dates (usually dates of the founding of existing university departments, institutes, and societies). This conveniently excludes those colleagues and ancestors of ours of the 17th and 18th centuries (Malthus, Locke, Hume, Adam Smith, Lafitau, Montesquieu, Comte, *et al*) who were making empirical studies and generating broad theories which have at least as much relevance to behavioural science today as the speculations, theories, and experiments of Bernoulli, Lavoisier, Newton, Avogadro, Lamarck, and similar worthies have to modern chemistry, physics, and biology. It may be, of course, that while we are as old, we *are* less mature, than other sciences; such indeed might be a likely result of the fragmentation to which our field has been subjected. But I know of no demonstrably valid means of estimating the maturity of a science.

The myth of our scientific youthfulness seems at times to serve as a means of rationalizing to ourselves why it is not necessary to know what *has* been done ('because it can't amount to anything—we are a young science, you know'). It interlocks with provincialism which insists on coloured spectacles transmiting light waves only of the frequency of one's own discipline. Thus, with eyes hopefully fixed on the next stage of development, we often do not notice that our feet actually are planted on a considerable mound of data, of concept and theory, and of research technique; and if we do look down, we can perceive only the increment which our fellow-specialists have added.

*Brass Instruments and the Fear of Speculation.* Although it is a well-justified reaction against an era of verbose system-building, the anti-

124

speculative attitude of overly 'scientific' social scientists tend to limit research to those matters most obviously accessible to existing techniques. The basic principles of scientific method only too early can be confused with locally relevant techniques; and so we have our own 'brass instrument' traditions. In extreme cases this leads to a sort of intellectual *rigor mortis* (methodology is the rigour, and mortis is the dead body you have to cross to introduce into discussion any notion that cannot be tested by an existing technique).

The physical sciences are built in part on ambitious published speculations which waited, in some cases, for generations before empirical observation caught up with them. Behavioural scientists not infrequently, in an excess of devotion to the technical imago, insist on a sort of exposure-at-birth-on-a-windy-hillside for neonate hypotheses. This spartanism is not especially fertile of ideas or of inquiry into new areas, but it is extremely fertile of 'research design'. It leads to an interest, not in finding out, but in finding out how to find out (or how not to *be* found out). Sober and continuous, purposeful speculation about matters of fact and existence, either in conversation or in private thought, is often viewed as a sort of heresy or sin, manifestations of which are to be rigourously repressed, and of course *never* published. (Our texts in methods of behavioural research dwell at length on how to test hypotheses but have almost nothing to say concerning where the hypothesis comes from.) The demand that every hypothesis be put in immediately testable form begs the question of proof by implying that no kind of testing instrument not as yet developed can be expected to appear. If physics and chemistry had demanded the sort of immediate confirmation by existing experimental devices so often required by the behavioural scientist, there would have been no thermodynamics, no relativity, no atomic theory, virtually 'no nothing', including no new experimental equipment designed to answer unanswerable questions.

Fear of speculation may indeed lead to serious faults in research design. By a failure to speculate, to play with variables, to draw up complicated schemes, in both empirical and 'conceptual' formulations, the scientist may assume without awareness whole congeries of relationships which the simplest speculation would show to be at least questionable. Hence the possibility of the false analogy in experiment and the colossal overgeneralization that may attend it; hence the practice of making up a questionnaire in a week, and then spending years selecting the sample, administering the test, analyzing the data, and explaining the results; hence also the willingness to 'test' a very large theory (without really knowing what the theory is) by a simple empirical survey whose relevance is purely a matter of opinion, but whose reliability is extremely high. A science of human behaviour will not progress far which is not founded on a solid bedrock of enthusiastic speculation about raw data. Speculations about nature come first; *then* comes the systematic test of their descriptive value.

*Fear of 'Raw' Empiricism.* Venturing into the wilderness of facts, behavioural scientists sometimes succumb to a sort of arctic hysteria and become preoccupied with repeating magic words like 'hypothesis', 'concept', 'theory', and 'model'. While I have made strictures against the bleak spartanism of certain views of behavioural science, and shall complain later about restricting empiricism to too few phenomena, there should be no question that the natural history approach to human behaviour is indispensable, and in some ways the 'rawer' it is the better.

Speculation about 'raw facts' is the source of all hypothesis. Strangely enough, the speculator and the natural historian are closer to each other in many ways than is either to the methodologist or the systematic theorist who only too often is merely concerned with creating a science of definitions. The indispensable thing is an interest in the facts, and this, in their different ways, speculation and 'raw' empiricism share. Without a rich and ever-renewed body of raw empirical data about which to speculate, behavioural scientists would soon be reduced to regarding each others' hypothesis-tests as their sole source of empirical information about human behaviour; and since only data relevant to the hypothesis are recorded in the typical test of a hypothesis, the well would quickly run dry. Some methodologist would eventually propose that since all the scientist can *really* observe reliably are controlled laboratory situations, and since all he can conceive is deducible from existing hypotheses, the outside world may operationally be considered non-existent and behaviour outside the laboratory may be ignored by the behavioural scientist—thus stamping out raw empiricism forever.

*Fads and 'Group-mindedness'.* David Riesman in *The Lonely Crowd* puts his finger on a phenomenon which, to the extent that it occurs in science, may be subversive of progress. This is 'other-directedness': the proposition that one should let one's colleagues be one's guide. 'Other-directedness' is appropriate in some kinds of enterprise, perhaps, but has stultifying effects on basic scientific research, since it places a premium on conformity and convention. The scientist is, or should be, an independent fellow of high integrity who is guided by the data and his own imagination. This is an idealistic notion, but science is an idealistic avocation. Basic discoveries are rarely made by conventions; and choosing problem, theory, and methodology on the criterion of their acceptability to one's colleagues not infrequently results in a condition of the blind leading the blind.

'Group-mindedness' in this sense is fertile ground for faddism. There are many problems in the area of human behaviour which are for a time fashionable; on which a certain amount of work is done; and which are then dropped and almost forgotten, not because the problem was worthless or was solved, but because the fad changes. Social and cultural evolution is one such problem area virtually abandoned but by no means exhausted; the study of occupational types in sociology is another; the analysis of the processes of association in psychology is a third; the study of instincts, drives, or tensions is a fourth; the problem of 'psychic unity' has never really been pursued; and the list could be extended.

The logical consequence of the philosophy of the pack is both the frustration of innovation and the abandonment of classic problems before they have been solved. In such a climate, a science of human behaviour conceived as an organized discipline would have great difficulty in avoiding the fate of the fad.

*Depersonalization.* Related to 'group-mindedness' is a current tendency to depersonalize the subject matter of human behaviour. There are certain kinds of assumptions, almost impossible to verify, which are made on faith by any science and whose validity or invalidity does not become apparent until after a number of year. I think there is a set of such assumptions, widely subscribed to, in the behavioural sciences, which taken together amount to an operational denial of the reality of the individual and of the reality of phenomena whose locus is assumed to be an individual. 'The group' tends to become the unit of discourse and of observation, and the individual is seen largely as a function of group characteristics and of social interaction. The group rather than individual focus, increasingly prevalent not only in the social but even the psychological sciences, expresses itself in many symptomatic acts: in confusing the central tendency of a distribution with the distribution itself, in emphasizing 'adjustment to the group' rather than 'adjustment to one's own impulses', in the insistence on viewing social behaviour as 'role', and in repeatedly asserting that 'great men' do not make history; as well as in flat statements of the order, 'without the group, the individual is nothing' and 'an individual personality is merely the subjective aspect of a culture'.

Now such attitudes about 'individuality' are essentially philosophical postulates, and are beyond the reach of empirical verification or disproof.

Put abstractly, indeed, the assertion of individual or group determinism is almost meaningless. But such philosophies are rarely put abstractly, nor are attempts made to test them: they function as silent determinants of the sorts of phenomena to be considered, the kind of data to be collected, and how they are to be organized. The group-determinism assumption becomes part of the operational definition of 'human'.

As I have suggested, this assumption is in itself neither 'true' nor 'false': it is merely gratuitous. Its currency, however, and the way in which it fixes the student's attention, virtually unconsciously, on one thing to the exclusion of another, means that a science which among other things attempts to treat the individual *as* individual will have hard sledding.

### A SCIENCE OF HUMAN BEHAVIOUR

*Focus.* If a science of human behaviour is to be anything more than a concatenation of miscellaneous disciplines, specialities, and viewpoints, it must have its own focus of analysis. Such a focus should not *substitute* for existing foci, but should merely require that the existing partial behavioural sciences unite *when the new focus is being employed.* Some of the foci in cultural anthropology for example, are *culture* and *national character;* in psychiatry and clinical psychology, *individual personality;* in social psychology and sociology, the *characteristics of groups;* and so on. The science of human behaviour, if it is to be a separate field, needs a different focus from any of them, and one which *demands* the joint utilization of the resources of all the 'ancestral' disciplines.

At Chicago, an interesting experiment in interdisciplinary thinking has been going on. Concepts of information theory and thermodynamics are being used as a basis for a body of formulations about the principles governing the maintenance of equilibrium states, ranging from purely physical equilibria, through organic homeostatic mechanisms, to psychic and socio-cultural equilibrium systems. This focus—the mechanism of the steady state—is one very possible focus for a science of human behaviour.

Another possible focus for a science of human behaviour, and one which I should like to suggest, is the analysis of types of events. While the *data* of any of the behavioural sciences are largely derived from the observation of events, rarely are individual events or types of events (except in psychiatry and history) intensively studied in themselves; rather, a few aspects are abstracted for study. A behavioural event may be defined as a series of energy-transformations involving human organisms, the boundaries of which (susceptible of being plotted in time and space) are identifiable as breaks in a curve of energy-flow (the break being either a change in rate, direction, or mode of energy-output). To put it in terms of concrete examples, a war; a man's life; a psychotic episode; a courtship-and-marriage sequence; an acculturation history; a nativistic revival movement; a natural disaster; the rise and fall of a civilization, can all be regarded as types of behavioural events. Any given event of the above mentioned types, seen as a total *Gestalt*, for its adequate description requires observation and analysis from the standpoints of several of the disciplines as conventionally established; and no one discipline could adequately observe or describe such an event without to some extent taking the role of its neighbours.

That there are types of events it hardly seems necessary to argue. Nevertheless, the common-sense recognition of the existence of a class of events does not carry us far in the analysis of its characteristics and ranges of variability. From initial observations, it seems to me that it is possible to plot out dynamic structures characteristic for certain types of events which will be valid, in their general form, cross-culturally. Thus, for example, the disaster event may be charted both in terms of functional time and functional area around the point of maximum impact:

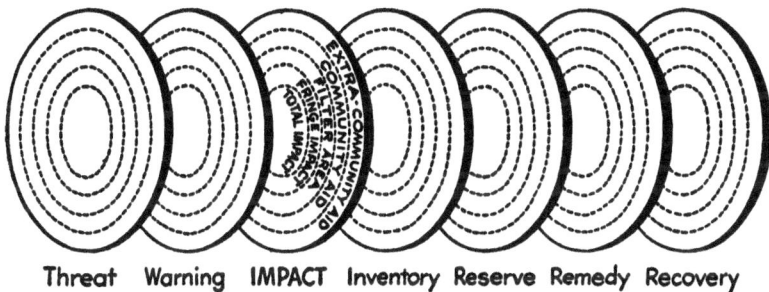

Threat    Warning    IMPACT    Inventory    Reserve    Remedy    Recovery

Any disaster area can be described in terms of the differential function, if any, of the persons in these various areas and at these various times with respect to the disaster. The schema does not require, for instance, that all 'filter area' persons act alike, whether white American, Japanese, or Eskimo; or even that every disaster necessarily have a filter area. Similarly, 'disaster time' can also be divided into categories: pre-disaster state, threat, warning, impact, inventory, rescue, remedy, recovery.[1] Behaviour of various orders—pertaining to communications, emotional reaction (the 'disaster syndrome'), transportation, relief activities, etc.— can be located in time and space, and, ideally at least, both generalizations about disasters as such, and classification of disasters into structural

---

[1] See John W. Powell, Jeannette Rayner, and Jacob E. Finesinger, 'Responses to Disaster in American Cultural Groups', in *Symposium on Stress*, Washington: Army Medical Service Graduate School, 1953.

129

types, can be accomplished. The extent of generalization, indeed, depends solely on the range of the cases for comparison, and the detail with which observations are made concerning various sorts of behaviour. In principle, this kind of approach is applicable to any type of human event: marriage, nativistic revival, war, group decision, etc. There are some additional implications, growing out of the use of energy-flow as the basis of the concept of event, which I should like to explore in other papers. At the moment, however, it is sufficient to point out that the orientation is not towards cross-sectional patterns or steady-state systems, but toward the *unsteady-state*, when things happen. The principle involved is that since *the payoff is in what actually happens,* a science of human behaviour should study directly the processes by which things of various kinds do happen, rather than the distribution of static characteristics.

*Holistic Empiricism.* Any type of event should, at least initially, be examined along all dimensions observably present. In practice, this means that at least the possibility of the relevance of the following dimensions must be considered: time; physical space and environment; personality structures and dynamics of participating individuals; cultures of groups, representatives of which participate in the event; actual networks of interpersonal relationships of participants, which may or may not be culturally defined; and distribution of demographic characteristics of participating individuals (age, sex, and the incidence of various other characteristics).

The science of human behaviour, like any science, is necessarily empirical in that it aims to describe observable phenomena. Scientific description, however, is not necessarily best achieved in every day language or concepts; and whether admitted or not, is invariably mediated by the logical, conceptual, and theoretical system of the observer. Much self-avowed empiricism in the social sciences has been so narrowly conceived, its techniques so arbitrary, and its underlying assumptions so much taken for granted, that it is an empiricism which leaves the empiricist very little to be empirical about. Holistic empiricism, precisely because of the multiplicity of variables recognized as operative in any event, requires formal, concrete, and explicit formulation of its guiding theories and assumptions.

*Pan-disciplinary Approach.* A corollary of the holistic principle is the pan-disciplinary nature of a science of human behaviour, at least in its initial stages. This implies an eclecticism of substance as well as of vocabulary.

130

Inter-disciplinary experiments, designed to break down barriers to communication, have been very popular in late years, but I think I should be safe in saying that there is a certain ambivalence about them: where once distance lent enchantment, familiarity has sometimes bred contempt. Part of such disillusionment as has developed has been, I suspect, owing to an initial over-estimation of the value of learning the vocabulary and concepts of one's scholarly neighbours. The intellectual millennium does not arrive when a mere semantic convention has been established. Learning the thought-ways of another science is a necessary but often tiresome chore, of no particular value in and of itself, and is comparable to learning to read a foreign language. One absorbs a small amount of information about various things in the process of learning to read a foreign language—but not much. And neither does the accumulation of a psychiatric vocabulary by, let us say, a sociologist, necessarily involve much knowledge of the phenomena with which psychiatry deals, or even an intention to acquire such knowledge.

By pan-disciplinary therefore I mean something more than achieving a common language; more than that platonic antenna-rubbing known as 'cross-fertilization'; more than the 'team approach' (which so often either approaches only the least common denominator of ideas in the group, or else the ideas of one discipline carried out with very low efficiency by the adherents of others). The necessity here is that specialists sitting in interdisciplinary conference accept, to a *greater* degree, than they do their own, the findings of fact and arguments of theory of other disciplines, until such time as they have worked in that discipline and can regard it as one of their own specialties.

This reduces to two principles of pan-disciplinary work: the abandonment of the reduction-to-a-common-denominator philosophy, and acceptance and utilization of the knowledge of the various disciplines in their own terms; and the preservation of these disciplines (or essential parts of them) as specialties in the larger science of human behaviour. The behavioural scientist should in the beginning understand and utilize anthropology, history, sociology, psychoanalysis, etc. as they stand, rather than attempt to formulate watered-down and distorting combinations of content and research procedure. This applies also to training. Parallelism of disciplines with mutual acceptance, and for some individuals, specialized knowledge in several, should be the rule, rather than 'cocktail integration' in the sense of diluted versions of each mixed together in an interdepartmental shaker.

*Anthony F. C. Wallace*

1. Human behaviour has always been a fascinating subject for human beings. We observe ourselves, our families, our associates in work and play. We form opinions about all of them, we approve or disapprove of their actions, we reprove those we disapprove of. We learn to base our own activities on the expected reactions of others. We lay down explicit rules of conduct, and we teach ourselves and our children to follow them. In these ways, an 'art' of culture has always existed. Human beings have had to practise this art in order to exist. Some have done it well, others less well. But only the non-survivors have done badly, for the very fact of surviving means that somehow one knows how to get along with somebody, somewhere, some of the time.

In the past century, there has gradually grown up in the field of human behaviour a body of scientific doctrine. As in other fields, the practitioners of this one have started from common knowledge, have used common sense, and have tried to arrive at statements which will describe the patterns of behaviour and the relations between them. These various statements are gathered together under various names, indicating the specific orientation or interest of the observer: sociology, social psychology, ethnology, cultural anthropology, linguistics, folklore. Ancillary to all such work have been studies of man's biology—physical anthropology; studies of material remains of past societies—archaeology; and the various special studies of certain activities of our own society that go under the name of 'the humanities'. The general term anthropology has been used to cover all or most of these fields of study, and we shall use it here.

In our meaning, anthropology is the study of human culture in all its ramifications. Culture can be defined as the learned and shared behaviour by means of which human beings interact in societies. Anthropology in this sense then includes the examination of language and communication in general, of social structure, of how human beings subsist, of the relations between men and women, of the basic controlling situational factors of environment and the passage of time, of what and how people learn, of rest and play and diversion, of the ways in which people defend their mental and physical well-being, and of the artifacts men make and what they do with them. Kept in mind constantly is the biological base—the fact that we are a species of animal.

2. Not all the practitioners of all the fields mentioned have considered themselves anthropologists. But those who have have consciously striven to construct a science. The methods pursued have been largely informal and personal, as was to be expected in a field of such wide extent and diversity. The learning of techniques from field experience has been emphasized. Ethnologists have reported the details of interpersonal contacts, linguists have actually learned to speak many languages, archaeologists have insisted on the necessity of handling the actual artifacts. All of them have largely avoided the building of frames of references. This stems chiefly from the pragmatism of the whole of American culture. In anthropology as such it continues the tradition set by Boas: the blows he dealt to the evolutionary thinking of Morgan and others succeeded in keeping down all other attempts at conceptual schemes for many years. A corollary has been that many anthropologists have looked down on those of their associates with little or no field experience. In this connection, the attitude towards linguists is instructive: those linguists who worked with 'primitive' informants were admitted to the fold; those who worked on languages of so-called civilized peoples were not; and yet a moment's thought shows that all working with a language at first hand is necessarily 'field work'—the actual gathering of data direct from the source.

The informal attitudes and the personal diversity have brought about the overlooking of certain kinds of data, and have made comparison between material from different cultures difficult. But on the other hand the workers in the field have given attention to minute detail and technical accuracy in what they did study, so that vast quantities of precise information about human behaviour, past and present, have been accumulated.

3. As the amount of data has grown, more and more practitioners of the various anthropological sciences have felt the need for conceptual frames in which to situate their findings, and—even more necessary—in terms of which to conduct their observations.

The informality and rapport between the anthropologist and his informant have been seen to be not enough to insure the obtaining of comparable and checkable data. The long lists of details were often meaningless, because no one could see the patterns into which they fell, and all too seldom did all the items in a list belong to equivalent orders of phenomena.

Shy away as they must from rigid conceptual schemes—being members of a sub-culture (American anthropologists stemming from the Boas tradition) that holds such schemes to be of little value—they nonetheless had to do something about the situation. The linguists, led by Sapir, began to concern themselves about the structural significance of their findings. Anticipating the Prague school of phonemicists, Sapir in 1925 laid down some general principles that have been followed since. Even before that American linguists were trying to formalize their field of science: Bloomfield in 1916 was analyzing Tagalog much as he analyzed Menomini a generation later. And, of course, Boas in all his work had a conceptual framework for linguistic analysis that differed little from what is done today.

Archaeologists have from time to time sought to develop conceptual frames for their work. Ethnologists have talked about themes, and about traits and trait-complexes. Sociologists have tried to make precise the notion of institutions. Psychologists and psychiatrists, and anthropologists oriented in their direction, have focussed their attention on personality and its characteristics.

With the entrance of anthropologists into public service at the time of World War II the need for explicit formalization of the field became pressing. Since the war all the practitioners of the field have been concerned with these theoretical problems, and to some extent have neglected the gathering of new data because of this situation. Meanwhile, linguistics, on the basis of Sapir's and Bloomfield's statements, has developed an analytical firmness unparalleled in the other fields. In linguistics one knows one's units, and the groups and patterns that they enter into. As more and more linguistics have become aware of the fact that they are anthropologists, more and more other anthropoligists have realized once more (seventy years after Boas first made it clear) that, as language is the key to the rest of culture, so linguistics is the model for the rest of cultural analysis.

4. The present authors, one working in linguistics, the other in cultural anthropology and archaeology, found when they began to collaborate in presenting integrated language-and-area programs, that their thinking about theory had been running along converging lines. The need for systematization of data in terms of precise technical definitions, and then for the formalization of these into working principles of wide application, was imperative. Working together to see what kind of analytical procedures could be applied, they concluded that the general methodology of linguistic analysis could be extended to other areas of culture if one recognized that culture was firmly grounded in biology, was a constellation of many systems like language, and was analyzable by finding the basic units of each such system and the groups and patterns into which the units are arranged.

5. The authors' experience in their fields has confirmed the principle that training for foreign service—diplomatic, consular, commercial, technical, etc.—is training in intercultural communication, and that the latter is brought about by the learner's becoming conversant with the total patterns of behaviour of the peoples he is to deal with. Languages must be learned as practical, usable means to such an end, but along with the language as such must go an understanding of its structure, knowledge of gestures and other communicative accompaniments of language, and comprehension of at least the main outlines of the structure of the rest of the culture, with knowledge of pertinent details such as class structure, kinship, position of women, economic status, resources, political institutions, and so on. General linguistics, and linguistic analysis of specific languages, are thus a part of the program. Anthropological theory must also be presented, with emphasis on specific cultures as they would be met with by the persons being trained.

In 1950 it became possible to work out in considerable detail the basic analysis of gesture and body-motion systems as communication—kinesics. Here at last was a cultural system that could be described in terms analogous to those used in linguistics. We now felt certain that our approach was valid, and we began to look for other systems.

We soon concluded that the criteria for a cultural system were these: the behaviour events in it must be clearly derivable from the biological nature of the human organism; they must be events of the same order; they must reflect and be reflected in other systems of the same kind. With this as a guide, we examined the biological nature of human beings as a basis for culture, and concluded that the fields of activity that were listed above in 1 (communication, social structure, subsistence or work, sex, space, time, learning, play, defence, exploitation [use of materials]) constitute an inclusive summary of the bases of culture. Wanting to arrive eventually at analyses that, following the linguistic model, would give us basic units, we worked out an analytical system that we presented in a prepublication edition.[1] A statement of the nature of this analysis—with the corrections and additions we have made since[2] appears below in 8. In all of this work, and in the work on kinesics, Henry Lee Smith, Jr., was of constant assistance, so much so that he should really be called a collaborator and co-author. Others of our colleagues also contributed much of value.

6. In linguistic analysis it has long been known that one must analyze the sounds of a language, then the grammatical forms into which the sounds are combined, and then the patterns in which the forms are arranged.[3] This general procedure has been followed for centuries—the Sanskrit grammarians having been particularly adept at it before modern times. During the 19th century the biological basis of linguistic analysis was explored by the phoneticians, and this work continues, and has expanded into acoustic studies in recent years. By the end of the first quarter of the 20th century it became clear that what had been done intuitively by earlier grammarians, including the devisers of writing systems, was to classify the sounds of speech into significant structure points. Sapir clarified and elaborated on this method, which had been in part anticipated by others (above, 3). Thus was defined the field of phonology, with its subdivisions of phonetics and phonemics. As phonology became more precise, it became possible to work on the grammatical forms more objectively—to do morphemics too in terms of structure and not in terms of 'meaning'. The precise delimitation of the subfields of morphemics—morphology and syntax—made it possible for the first time to see the relation of various phenomena such as 'tone of voice', gesture, voice quality, and others, to language as such. On the

---

[1] E. T. Hall, Jr., and G. L. Trager, *The Analysis of Culture*, American Council of Learned Societies, Washington, D.C., 1953.
[2] G. L. Trager, E. T. Hall, Jr., and D. H. Hunt, *Technical Aspects of the Analysis of Culture*, unpublished.
[3] See G. L. Trager, *The Field of Linguistics*, Occasional Paper 1, supplement to *Studies in Linguistics*, 7, 1949.

linguistic model, an analysis of gestures was made.[1] By this time the criteria for a cultural system mentioned in 5 above were apparent; we could then be sure of our limitation of language to certain kinds of phenomena, and had a guide to the classification of the phenomena excluded from language. We also saw that 'meaning', assigned to meta-linguistics,[2] was to be handled by the examination of the interrelations of cultural systems.

7. If cultural systems as a whole and severally are parallel to language, analysis of them must identify the units of each succeeding level of complexity. Then the grouping of these units into larger entities—sets—must be found and the several orders of such entities determined. Finally the patterning of the arrangements of the basic units and sets must be discovered. When a system has been described in this way, then it is possible to state its relations and those of any of its parts to other systems, point for point.

By such a procedure, such items as traits and trait-complexes can be pinned down. In working with kinship systems, for instance, one must find the basic units of relationship, and then determine what combinations of them enter into the structure of the system. If one is examining social structure, one must separate out class and caste and government and see what are the entities in each. If one is studying technology, one must find the analogs of phonemes and morphemes in artification. Proceeding along these lines, we arrived at an overall classification of culture and cultural systems, and have come to see, in general outline, how further analysis must go (references in 5).

8. When we concluded that culture is based on the ten basic phases of human behaviour that we listed above (5), we constructed a series of diagrams and elaborated from them a kind of proto-mathematics—as yet expressed largely in ordinary language rather than by special symbols. The detail of these constructions is to be found in the *Technical Aspects. . .* article mentioned above (5). Here we can only indicate the kinds of results achieved.

Using a two-dimensional diagram in which the ten phases served as both sets of coordinates, once as primary (designated by noun terms), and once as secondary, (adjectival terms), we got 100 intersections of a primary and a secondary phase. These intersections we call cultural systems. The ten cultural systems formed by the intersection of a phase

---

[1] R. L. Birdwhistell, *Kinesics*, Foreign Service Institute, U.S. Department of State, 1951.
[2] Trager, 1949, *op. cit.*

with itself are the basic systems of culture; these we have designated by the following terms: symbolics, society, operations, the sexes, space, time, enculturation, recreation, protection, pragmatics.

Examination of these basic systems, and of the possible content of the other ninety systems, led us to see that the basic phases can be paired. Interaction and exploitation are closely connected as extensions of the person behaving in the culture; symbolics includes language and other communication, and pragmatics include technology—the making of artifacts. Association and defence are both pattern *par excellence*; society includes government, class and caste, kinship; protection includes military defences, health practises, dealings with the supernatural. Work and play are activity: operations include all occupational and subsistence behaviour; recreation includes fun, games, joking. Bisexuality and learning are transformation: the system of the sexes includes maturation as a man or a woman, and enculturation includes education and rearing. Territoriality and temporality are situation; the systems of space and time deal with situation by measuring and weighing it, so to speak. Systems outside of the ten basic ones show various kinds of relationships; society and defence are related by virtue of being the basic systems in a pair of basic phases of activity; the system formed by association and defence in one combinatory order includes administration, and that by the other combinatory order includes law; all four of these are especially related as against all others.

The systems including the aspects of a pair of phases appear, in a circular diagram which we use, as concentric rings. Each such ring of systems is conceived of as composed of three concentric rings: the centre one involves the cultural activities based on basic units of the systems, the outer one deals with the sets into which these group, the inner ring involves the patterns of sets and units. The further significance of these types of units and groups is discussed in 9 below.

The criss-crossing of the three-fold subdivision of the phases of activity in the rings leads to a division of each system into nine fields. In symbolics we have arrived at some idea of the content of the fields, and may use them for illustration. (In the diagram the numbers are for reference only; they are taken from the complete analysis.)

The three fields given names are basic to all culture. Cerebration evaluates the sets of phenomena in the universe about us; how it works we can only guess, as yet. Coding differentiates the units or isolates of symbolic activity, probably in binary fashion. Communication combines these, along with material from the other fields (see below) into patterns. Communication is further subdivided. The three fields designated as 005, 007, 009 deal with the recognition of emotion and its expression in such things as the set of the voice and its qualities. The remaining

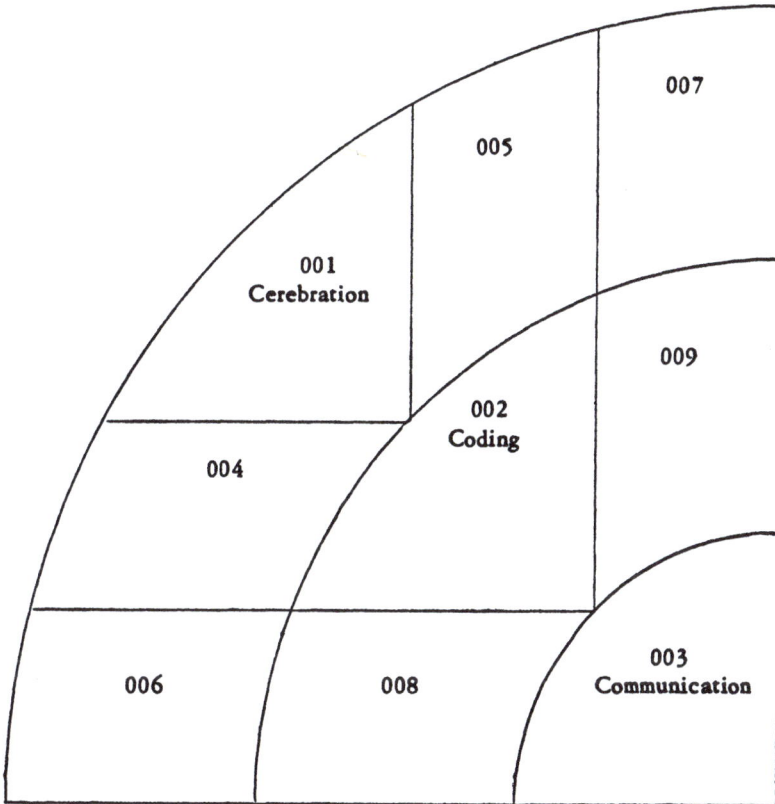

FIGURE 6. Fields of Symbolics.

fields, 004, 006, 008, deal with values and feelings, as expressed in body set and movement quality.

In each cultural system the field that deals with patterns and is analogous to communication (003) in symbolics can be further subdivided, in a manner like the division into fields, into nine foci. For communication this gives us the situation depicted in Figure 7. At this point it needs to be explicitly stated that the nine foci are grouped into three groups of three, just as are the fields (a grouping implied by the discussion above).

The focal axis 0031, 0032, 0033 constitutes the complex known as language. The phones are the basic units or isolates, the morphs are the sets of isolates, the context is the patterning of these, along with the effects from the two other groupings, the peripheries. The individual focal periphery, vocalization, consists of 0035, 0037, 0039; vocal differentiators are the communication systems employing laughing, crying,

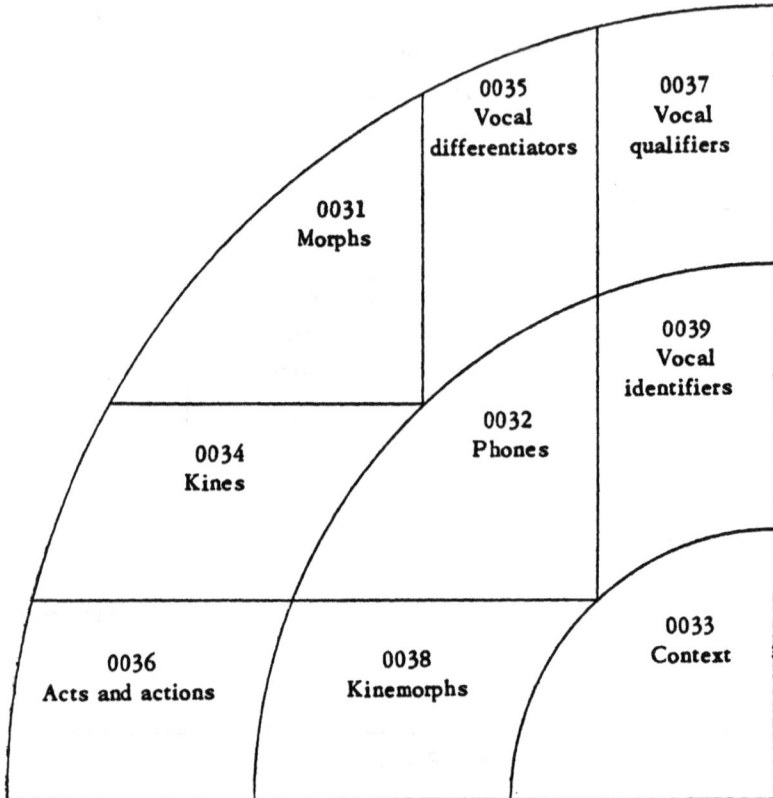

FIGURE 7. The Foci of Communication.

whispering, overall nasalization, and others as yet not specifically recognized by us; vocal qualifiers are the so-called tone-of-voice effects: over-loudness, over-softness, drawl, clipping, overhigh pitch, overlow pitch, rasp, openness, singing, monotone, and possibly a few others. The group focal periphery, kinesics, consists of 0034, 0036, 0038; kines are the units of gesture, evaluated as communication; acts and actions are the gesture patterns, similarly evaluated; kinemorphs are the gesture patterns differentiated as such.

The kind of subdivision described for symbolics has been worked out for society and enculturation also, though we have been less sure in assigning content and labels. Altogether there are envisaged 3775 systems, fields, subfields, foci, axes, and peripheries in the whole analysis. That is, there may be that many separate fields of investigation or disciplines in the field of anthropology as a whole, each perhaps as complex as linguistics.

9. In discussing the apprehension of cultural data, we have implied a classification into three types of units—sets, isolates, and patterns, and have alluded to three processes for treating the units—evaluation, differentiation, identification. Further elucidation of these types and processes is in point.

A set is a unit which is known to have constituent parts but which is treated as a whole at some levels. An isolate is an indivisible unit, one of the constituents of a set; of course, at some entirely different level, by reduction out of the field in terms of biology or physics, it may be subdivided. A pattern is an arrangement of sets and isolates. Evaluation determines whether A is greater or less (by appropriate standards of measurement) than B. Differentiation determines whether A is the same as B or not; this is the basic process in cultural analysis—asking the informant whether things are the 'same' or not. Identification describes in detail and specifies.

Sets, and evaluation, are said to be formal. Isolates, and differentiation, are informal. Patterns, and identification, are technical. Formal cultural behaviour connotes the traditional, the ideals, the means whereby a group maintains its solidarity and uniqueness, the things 'everybody knows', the standards that everyone is expected to uphold and impose on others and to resent the violation of. Informal behaviour connotes the situational, the things taken for granted and out of awareness, the individual adaptation to the formal, the things learned by observation and without 'thinking' about them. Technical behaviour involves the precise and describable, the emotionally unchanged, the new, the efficient, the things taught by a teacher (an expert) to a learner (a novice).

It is seen from this that in each cultural system its field axis consists of the field of evaluation of sets—purely formal, that of differentiation of isolates—purely informal, and that of identification of patterns—purely

141

technical. The technical field is the one that is again divided, and its focal axis—such as language in communication—has a formal, an informal, and a technical focus. The other groupings of fields and of foci are mixed, containing elements of different types. In language, as apparently elsewhere, the formal events—morphs—are learned first; then the isolates, the informal events—phones—are differentiated; and finally the technical patterns are acquired. In kinesics, the kines (evaluation of isolates) are apprehended first, but informally; the acts and actions are then acquired (as evaluation of patterns) and finally kinemorphs are isolated out (differentiation of patterns).

In cultural change the threefold division into formal, informal, and technical is extremely important. The formal parts of a culture cannot be changed by forthright attack by outsiders; they change only as a result of change from within. Informal culture is changed by being brought into awareness. Technical culture is easily changed by specific instruction and introduction of new techniques. A formal system is adapted to by individuals creating their informal reactions to it. With time some of these come into awareness and become technicalized. As the technical expands or changes it becomes the basis for new formal systems and the process is repeated.

10. We have now come, by a long road, to our title. The world is inhabited by some two and a half billion people. These are grouped into hundreds of societies, some large, some very small, each with its own culture. Cultures are found to be classifiable into culture areas. Depending on how closely one analyzes, there may be many or few such areas. We can, if we wish, speak of 'Western culture', and ignore the diversities among three-quarters of a billion people. Or we can break Western culture down into subtypes: Northern Europe, Central Europe, Southern Europe, Eastern Europe (or one can do this otherwise—Western Europe, Central Europe, Eastern Europe—with different boundaries), English-speaking North America, Latin America, Australia and New Zealand, South Africa, the Soviet world, the newer Westernized countries, and so on. Each of these can then be further subdivided. Whatever we do, the problem of communication is always there. And this communication, centering around language, involves everything in the cultures sooner or later. The citizen of the United States in Canada is rarely reminded of cultural differences; but let him try to fill his gasoline tank with 14 Imperial gallons when it will only hold 14 United States gallons, and he immediately begins to be disturbed, as he is when he looks for a green box in which to deposit his letter home and finds instead a red one. As

language differences increase, and as other cultural differences increase with them, the difficulties are recognized. But nowhere—or hardly anywhere—is there any recognition of what needs to be done about it.

Cultures must be analyzed as vastly complex systems, and each system and sub-system must first be analyzed in and of itself. The formal systems must be recognized and stated, the informal adaptations charted, and the technical elaborations described in detail. As anthropologists develop their knowledge of these things, they must be aware that all of culture is a kind of symbolization. Man interprets the universe through his senses, which are means of symbolizing (converting into symbols, that is) the impressions that his physical self receives. This being the nature of culture, it is understandable that the most explicitly symbolizing systems—those of communication, especially language, should always have been most easily acquired and should now constitute the organizational models for the scientist seeking to analyze culture. Linguistic analysis becomes thus the key to all cultural analysis, as a methodology. For language, as a cultural complex, reflects all the rest of culture, and since we know something about how to analyze it, we need but to follow its lead to see how to begin to study all other cultural behaviour. It has been suggested by the late B. L. Whorf[1] that language not only reflects all the rest of culture but actually affects our analysis of the universe about us by fitting it into the limitations of the linguistic structure: language is a sort of set of spectacles through which we see the world. This may be only partly true, but the pertinence of the linguistic model for the analysis of culture as a whole is all the greater to the extent that such influence exists.

It will have been noted that our treatment of culture has not included reference to personality or to institutional behaviour as such. We hold that the totality of human behaviour is threefold; there is the cultural constellation, discussed above; then there is the personality constellation —the province of the psychologist; and then there is the institutional constellation. We do not know how these differ, or even whether they may not all be different aspects of a single thing. But we know that they are related and connected in some way. Culture, being learned and shared, traditional, and inescapable, is the formal member of this threesome. Personality is a given, the means whereby the individual carries out his culture; it is the informal member. Institutions are the result of group activity stemming from the collective personality of the members of the group behaving in terms of the culture; it is the technical member.

---

[1] B. L. Whorf, *Collected Papers on Metalinguistics*, Foreign Service Institute, U.S. Department of State, 1952.

143

With this final extension of our scientific range of sight, we see that the content of such a term as metalinguistics can be extended to cover all the manifestations of communicative behaviour. The gesture, the specific vowel, the inelegant word, tie up with the clothes, the religion, the manners, and so on, of the individual or the group. The aim of inter-cultural communication becomes the understanding not only of culture in all its ramifications, but also of individual personality and of the dynamics of group behaviour. [14]

*George L. Trager and Edward T. Hall, Jr.*

Recently while preparing a radio broadcast on the poetry of company presidents, I looked at some of the morticians' trade journals, particularly *Casket and Sunnyside*. I anticipated a rich source here, but I was mistaken. For though the poetic efforts of successful business men are simple enough (rhymes are often achieved by mispronouncing words and metre by substituting hyphens for extra syllables), all advocate three principles, the last of which must be unacceptable to undertakers. They advocate faith in our economic system, in religion and in the human body; their message is two-fold: keep your bowels open and your mouth shut.

Doubts about the body's ability to solve all of its own problems may have discouraged morticians from entering this field. Certainly it can't be from pessimism, for they appear as a jolly lot, not consoling as in street car ads, but pleased. There's a humour column called 'Grave and Gay', and there are short stories, showing that undertakers have their own way of seeing things. In one about a broken marriage, the villain 'was slim and wore his clothes well—a dark overcoat with velvet collar set off by a white-silk muffler, dull-polished black shoes, gray gloves. In one hand he held a black derby hat, a tightly furled umbrella swung

# Has this happened to you . . . ?

15⁻

"It was a coronary thrombosis case . . . quite routine . . . at first. We received the body at 4:10 P.M., July 31. Preparations were completed and the body dressed and placed in the casket at 10:00 A.M., August 1. The family viewed the remains that afternoon and were very pleased with the results. At 6:00 P.M. the body was checked again. Appearance was very satisfactory. AND THEN . . .

## HAVE YOU EVER FELT LIKE YOU HAD SWALLOWED YOUR TONGUE?

Well, that's the feeling I had when I was called back to the funeral home at 11:00 P.M. and found we had a case of Tissue Gas with a capital "T". The gaseous condition was present over the head, scalp, trunk and legs down to the knees. We had a seemingly impossible task and in view of the fact that the deceased had a son being flown home from Korea, we knew that some drastic action had to be taken . . . at once.

Cosmetics and clothing were removed. The body was then injected hypodermically with undiluted B&G TRIGG Cavity Fluid from 29 points. Three times during the next 24 hours the body was checked, massaged and reinjected. At 9:00 A.M., the following day, cosmetics were reapplied, the body dressed and casketed. The family viewed the body again and expressed the opinion that it looked as good, if not better than when they had first viewed it.

The funeral was held 4 days later . . . 8 days after death. We felt this was quite an accomplishment but the credit is not ours.

*We merely placed TRIGG at the most advantageous points where it could 'Go to Work' ".*

**It doesn't cost to use B&G — It pays!**

Let TRIGG go to work for you too . . . not only on the unusual cases, but in any case.

# B & G PRODUCTS CO.

308 PRINCE STREET — ST. PAUL 1, MINN.

146

from the crook of his other arm. But a second look showed signs of considerable effort taken to tighten the sagging lines of his face—sessions with hot towels and massage creams vigorously applied. The underlying hardness of his face showed through the careful "conditioning" of expert barbers.'

The best writing appears in the advertisements: ARTISTIC EXPRESSION THROUGH THE YEARS WITHOUT THOUGHT OF SELFISH RETURN; I'VE USED FRIGID FLUID FOR 29 YEARS—I OUGHT TO KNOW; TROUBLE WITH TRUNK CAVITIES?; LOOK OUT FOR HUMPTY-DUMPTY REACTIONS; MALE BODIES NEED COSMETICS, TOO; REGAIN THE COMPLEXION OF LIFE; It seemed like just the other day you first took your son to school. Soon he'll be coming home with all sorts of wonderfully exciting things to talk about. Just like you, those first days you were learning your profession as a funeral director. Like the time you discovered that. . . .

Academics generally limit their reading to scholarly books and thus ignore the bulk of printed material. Magazines, mail-order catalogues, trade journals, university presidents' reports, Who's Who—what Siegfried Giedion calls 'anonymous history'—are never reviewed, presumably because they are regarded as neither literary nor scholarly. Nowadays there's much talk about the threat of the new media to print, upon whose monopoly of knowledge the health of Western letters is alleged to depend. Usually the conflict is cast in terms of *Paradise Lost* vs. comic books. Before the argument is closed, it would be well to consider all forms of print.

*Rev. Doctor H. J. Chaytor,* 3 St. Paul's Road, Cambridge, retired three years ago as Master of St. Catherine's College, Cambridge University. He is the author of *A Companion to French Verse, The Troubadors of England,* and *From Script to Print,* W. Heffer and Sons, from which his article is taken.

*Kamo Chomei's Hojoki* is one of the standard classics of Japan. Although every Japanese reads it as a schoolchild and several missionary translations have been printed in Japan, it has never been adequately made known to the West. Its sub-title, *A Fugitive Essay,* is a direct translation.

*Thomas Rowe* served for five years in Tokio as Chief-of-Documents, Translation, for the Intelligence Section of General Headquarters of the Far East. He is now in Europe producing documentary films.

*Anthony Kerrigan* has dedicated the *Hojoki* translation to Antonia Gurevitz-Kerrigan. Editor and translator of several books, mainly dealing with Hispanic-American history, and author of one book of verse, he is a graduate of the Military Intelligence Service Japanese Language School, has worked on films in Europe, and now owns an art gallery at 106 East Oak Street, Chicago.

*Dr. Martha Wolfenstein* is a psychoanalyst and co-author of *Movies: A Psychological Study.*

*Ray L. Birdwhistell* is Coordinator of an Interdisciplinary Committee on Culture and Communication, University of Louisville.

*Dorothy Lee* is now at Ann Arbor.

*Kenneth MacLean* is Professor of English, Victoria College.

*I. Potekin and M. Lewin* are Assistant Directors, Miklukho-Maklai Institute of Ethnography, Academy of Sciences of the USSR.

*Harold A. Innis*, late Dean of the Graduate School, University of Toronto, was the author of *The History of the Canadian Pacific Railway, The Fur Trade in Canada*, and *The Cod Fisheries.*

*W. H. McCulloch*, 38 Lomond, Road, Edinburgh, is a junior official in the Department of Health for Scotland. 'As a result of personal experience while a student at Cambridge, I have given continual thought for the last fifteen years or so to the place which narcissism and doublegoing have in the suicidal process. D. S. Savage and Louis Adeane read the manuscript and offered valuable criticism.'

*Anthony F. C. Wallace*, Assistant Professor of Sociology, University of Pennsylvania, is the author of *Teedyuscung* and *The Modal Personality of the Tuscarora Indians*. His article was written while he was a Fellow of the Social Science Research Council.

*George L. Trager*, Institute of Languages, Georgetown University, is a co-author of *Outline of English Structure* and *Outline of Linguistic Analysis.*

*Edward T. Hall, Jr.*, anthropologist with the Foreign Service Institute, Department of State, is a co-author of *An Analysis of Culture.*

The moon mask on the cover is a Northwest Coast Indian one. The picture was supplied by Crawley Films and Imperial Oil Limited.

The drawing on page 77 is by Gert Pollmer of the Canadian Broadcasting Corporation.

www.ingramcontent.com/pod-product-compliance
Lightning Source LLC
Chambersburg PA
CBHW071100280326
41928CB00050B/2577